ROAMING WITH THE RYLONS AUSTRALIA AND NEW ZEALAND

18 DAYS IN SYDNEY, MELBOURNE, AND THE NORTH ISLAND

JAYNE RYLON

HAPPY ENDINGS PUBLISHING

Copyright © 2019 by Jayne Rylon

All rights reserved.

No part of this book may be reproduced or shared in any form or by any electronic or mechanical means—including email, file-sharing groups, and peer-to-peer programs—without written permission from the author, except for the use of brief quotations in a book review.

If you have purchased a copy of this ebook, thank you. I greatly appreciate knowing you would never illegally share your copy of this book. This is the polite way of me saying don't be a thief, please and thank you!

If you're reading this book and did not purchase it, or it was not purchased for your use only, then please purchase your own copy. Refer to the don't-be-a-thief section above for clarification. :)

eBook ISBN: 978-1-941785-97-3

Print ISBN: 978-1-941785-98-0

Photography: Jayne Rylon

Cover Art: Jayne Rylon

Editing: Mackenzie Walton

Proofreading: Fedora Chen

Version 7

ABOUT THE BOOK

Pack a bag and let's go! Join Jayne and her husband, the reluctantly adventurous Mr. Rylon, for the trip of a lifetime in this casual and frank guidebook with a twist. Whether you're planning a vacation of your own or want to experience an exotic and remote destination from the comfort of your own armchair, you've come to the right place.

This book includes:

- **A Step By Step Itinerary** – 18 days are detailed for you including what to do, how to get there, and where to stay
- **Maps, Images, and Companion Vlogs** – Sometimes a picture is worth a thousand words. See the highlights for yourself through Jayne's photography and over an hour of videos that give you more context for the details included in the book.
- **Budget Breakdown** – Jayne used to be a financial analyst before writing full-time. She's put her spreadsheets to good use tracking costs at the lowest level so you'll know where you can save or splurge.
- **Restaurant Reviews** – Jayne and Mr. Rylon tried a wide variety of cuisines from street meat to five-star gourmet restaurants so you can find something you'll enjoy as much as they did.
- **Rylon Recommendations** – Tips and tricks to help you make the most of your vacation.
- **Areas Covered** – Sydney, Blue Mountains, Melbourne, Great Ocean Road, Auckland, Waitomo, Taupo, Rotorua, Matamata, Tauranga, Whitianga, Hot Water Beach, Coromandel, Takapuna

DEDICATION

To the long-suffering Mr. Rylon for surviving many rounds of Vacation Boot Camp.

And especially for Mom, Dad, and Kolin.
I finally wrote a book you're allowed to read!

FOREWORD

Welcome to Vacation Boot Camp! Okay, that's not really what I have in store for you. But that's how my husband, affectionately known as Mr. Rylon, likes to describe my desire to see as much as possible when we're visiting some new corner of the world.

As a *New York Times* & *USA Today* bestselling author of over fifty romance novels, I've been fortunate enough to travel often for research, book signings, and reader conferences. Poor Mr. Rylon has gotten dragged along, too.

Despite his grumbling, I'm pretty sure he secretly enjoys exploring with me as long as I don't go overboard with my planning. Here's where this guide comes in. You might as well put my labor to good use, right?

It'll be win-win. Fun for me, combining my love of writing with my passion for adventures around the globe. Less trouble for you, skipping grueling hours hunting for information. Even if you're a Mr. Rylon and decide not to do everything we jammed into these two-plus weeks, you'll have plenty to keep you occupied. Pick what sounds fun to you and try those things.

You see, I've scoured the internet while procrastinating from writing my fiction books. I searched for all the best places to see, things to do, where to stay, restaurants to eat at, and how to get there so you don't have to be bothered with the grunt work.

I'd say don't tell my editor, except she will have already fixed my mistakes in this guide by the time you read it. *Hi, Mackenzie!* Besides, I've missed enough deadlines that it's probably pretty obvious I was goofing off at least some of the time.

Foreword

Oh! I suppose I should also tell you that in my life prior to lounging in my pajamas while writing steamy romances, I had a "real" job. One that required me to wear actual pants and a bra and go out in the cold on winter days and crap like that.

I have a master's degree in finance, and used to be the manager of financial planning and analysis for a Fortune 500 company. I'm sharing this with you because I worked up a detailed budget and will share my actual costs for this itinerary as we traveled it.

Of course, you can drastically adjust how much you spend through the choices you make—either in favor of frugality or luxury—but it should give you a rough estimate of how much you need to fatten up your piggy bank if you choose to go on a journey like ours.

The budget will cover all aspects of our trip. However, if you have less time available or fewer vacation funds, you could eliminate certain segments of this itinerary. Therefore, I've broken the guide down into sections that roughly equate to a few days each in Sydney and Melbourne as well as a week in New Zealand.

Above all else, I want to make sure you know I'm not trying to be an expert on all things Australia and New Zealand. I'm relating my experiences and letting you know what I think worked, as well as what might have been improved.

It's often overwhelming for me to narrow down the options presented in a comprehensive guide and then group the activities that interest me into achievable daily chunks. So I'm taking a more focused approach. This is just one potential itinerary, the one I know about from my personal experiences and can share well. I hope it's one you'll enjoy, too.

Come along as I take you on our most recent trip to Australia and New Zealand. Be sure to check back for other destination guides in the future!

PART I

STUFF YOU NEED TO DO BEFORE YOU GO, AND GETTING THERE

Before we jump into the fun parts of vacationing, we need to take care of the stuff that's annoying and frustrating, which means you usually leave it until the last possible second. Yes, I'm talking about preparing for your trip and then —even worse—actually getting to your glorious destination, where all that aggravation will suddenly become worth it.

First things first. Assuming you live in the US, like I do, you're not going anywhere unless you first have a valid passport. You know that part. However, what I'd forgotten—because it's been nearly a decade since I went someplace (China) that requires one—you also need to arrange for a visa when traveling to Australia from most countries. Fortunately, the process is painless so long as you know to do it before you are en route.

On the Australian Government Department of Home Affairs website, there is a visa finder located at www.homeaffairs.gov.au/Trav/Visa-1 that will assist you in figuring out which visa you need to apply for. Most of you will be traveling for leisure and for less than three months, so you can apply for the Electronic Travel Authority, subclass 601 visa.

In order to qualify for this visa, you must hold a valid passport from an eligible nation and be outside Australia. Remember how I said this is straightforward as long as you do it before you get there? Don't forget!

The visa is valid for twelve months from the time you apply, and can be used for up to three months of travel in the country on each entry with multiple entries allowed. You're able to use this visa to visit family and friends, be a tourist, undertake business visitor activities (check the site for more details on what that entails), and study abroad so long as you don't exceed the time limits.

You can apply for the ETA online (www.eta.immi.gov.au/ETAS3/etas) for a $20 AUD fee. A decision will be emailed to you immediately afterward. The visa is tied electronically to your passport number so you don't need to bring anything with you, though I did print out a copy of our approvals just in case. For travel from countries other than the US and Canada, refer to the Australian Government website.

While we're on the topic of fees and costs for a moment, also be sure to check the exchange rate. You can do that at www.xe.com/currencyconverter. That way you'll know what you're getting yourself into when you see the cost of lodging or activities you book online, which will likely be quoted in AUD. Generally, this will be a benefit for travelers from the US as the Australian dollar has historically been valued lower than the US dollar.

I'll be citing the actual prices I paid in US dollars for the remainder of the guide because that's what's on my credit card or bank statements and easiest to look up. At the time we traveled to Australia, the exchange rate was $1AUD = 76¢ USD. This was a big help in reducing the cost of our trip and allowing us to splurge every now and again, especially when eating out.

Once your visa is approved, which I recommend taking care of before you book anything—especially anything nonrefundable—you should also consider whether or not you want trip insurance. Mr. Rylon and I are pretty cautious, so I do usually buy it for major travel.

The reason you need to decide this upfront is because most companies require that you purchase a policy within some number of days from when you make your first booking. I've used both TravelGuard (mvp.travelguard.com) and DAN travel insurance (www.diversalertnetwork.org/trip), which is offered through my SCUBA diving organization but covers more than just SCUBA diving or dive trips and is not restricted to DAN members. The mid-tier plan at each provider covers essentially the same things for the same price. The cost of your insurance is relative to the amount of coverage you need. To protect the amount we laid out for this trip, we paid $370 in insurance fees.

Sad/happy story time... A couple of days before the first international trip Mr. Rylon and I ever took together, to Ireland, my uncle passed away. I flew from our house in Ohio to New York to be with my family, and we had to postpone our vacation.

Mr. Rylon was able to rebook every single thing from flights to accommodations to attraction tickets, for one week later using assistance from an agent at the insurance company. They did this at no additional cost to us, during an extremely stressful time in our lives when neither of us would have been able to handle it on our own.

After that experience, we've never regretted buying travel insurance. As you'll see from the budget section, we spent roughly $16,000 on this trip. Even if you were exceptionally frugal, I don't think you could do it for much less than nine or ten thousand dollars due to airfare costs, which are a big chunk of the expenditure. In our case, they were nearly half the total cost of the trip and are nonrefundable. Therefore, a couple hundred bucks was well worth it for my peace of mind and to protect that investment. Nothing would suck more than missing out on the vacation of a lifetime than missing out and still having to pay for it all.

Okay... Insurance. Check. Or not check—up to you.

Now you need to decide *when* you're going to go. Here's my advice: check the weather! In our case, we traveled to Australia because I was invited to participate in a multi-author book signing in Melbourne on a specific date in September. In the southern hemisphere, this is very early spring. In Sydney temperatures were pleasant, ranging from 50-80°F. Farther south, in Melbourne, it had snowed the week before we were there and was a cold and rainy 40-55°F. For New Zealand, we stayed on the North Island, where we saw temperatures hovering around 55°F.

While I personally wouldn't enjoy sweating profusely while I was touring this region, which is definitely possible at certain times of the year, visiting another month or two later or during their autumn probably would have been ideal. So keep that in mind when you book. But if you're tied to a specific time of the year, as we were, you'll still have a great experience if you pack appropriately.

By *appropriately*, I don't mean that you should bring fourteen suitcases either.

Keep in mind that flights in Australia have different, stricter baggage policies than most US flights. If you're doing any train travel, they also have restrictions you'll need to consider. I personally pack very light and always make sure to look for a place to stay that offers laundry facilities so I can cut down on what I'm lugging around. Then again, I'm not the kind of person who owns ten pairs of shoes and, in fact, have been known to travel with only a pair of flip flops despite cool weather so...you do you, but be prepared to pay extra or be mailing yourself some excess items if you overpack.

Next, I would also say you need to do some research on where to go and what to do when you're finally on the other side of the world, but you're already reading this guide, so I think you've got that covered. I've (hopefully) weeded out some of the sludge so you can take a shortcut around this part of the planning process.

Finally, a note from the much more tech-savvy Mr. Rylon... Don't forget to pick up some international adapters for your electronics if you're coming from the US on this trip. In most cases, you can still use your same cords and power bricks (read them to make sure the input says something like 100/110-240 volts). However, you'll need adapters since the number and layout of the prongs accepted by the outlets will vary from country to country.

In addition to the adapter set, here are a few links to products we find to be worth the effort of hauling around. For the sake of transparency, these are affiliate links. If you click one and buy something, I get a small kickback. However, I'm only recommending products here that I personally use and love.

Travel Essentials

- Universal Travel Adapter – https://amzn.to/2qPEH7S
- Four-port Charger – https://amzn.to/2K6gSS0
- Wire Organizer – https://amzn.to/2HfuqN8
- Laptop (and more) Backpack – https://amzn.to/2HjYseO
- Squishable Hat – https://amzn.to/2JbGyeL
- Sunscreen – https://amzn.to/2JcGfQS
- Ultra Comfy (if not the prettiest) Shoes – https://amzn.to/2Jhw5i2
- Convertible Pants – https://amzn.to/2HVveUN
- Toiletry Kit – https://amzn.to/2HiAKDJ
- Packing Cubes – https://amzn.to/2F74Ier
- Suitcases – https://amzn.to/2JfjprM
- Kindle – https://amzn.to/2qPDAWk

Okay, whew! Now that you've taken care of all the boring, expensive, and frustrating junk, you're prepared for the fun to begin!

DAY 1 - LAX AND THE SANTA MONICA PIER

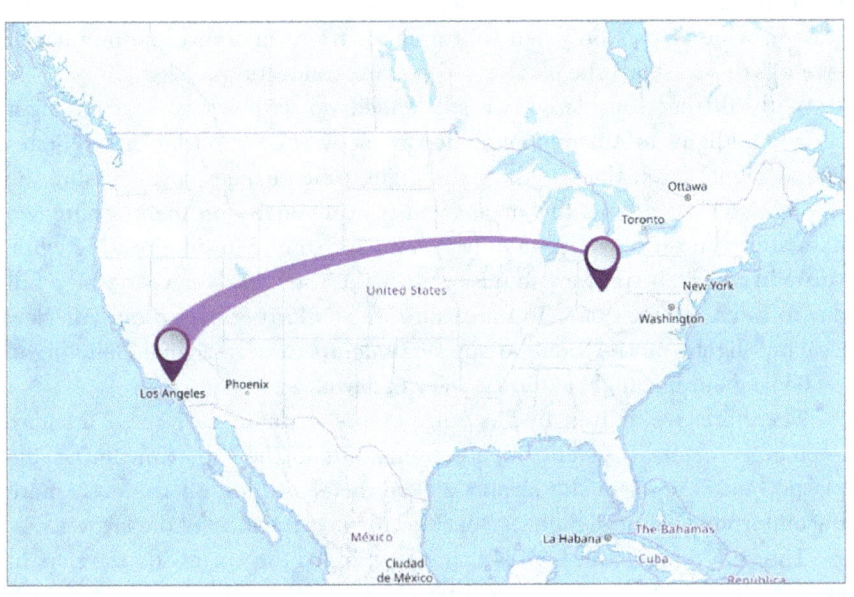

© OpenStreetMap contributors

Since this guide is based on my actual experiences making the trip from Columbus, Ohio in September of 2017, I'm going to talk about how we made our way across the country and then the Pacific. Obviously, this may or may not be relevant to you if you're approaching from an alternate origin. However, I hope some of my tips and tricks could be applicable regardless. It won't hurt my feelings if you skip to the juicy stuff...AKA arriving in Sydney.

The first thing you should know about Mr. Rylon and me is that despite our love for travel, we are risk-averse people—we have a lot in common with the hobbits we could imagine on the Hobbiton movie set we saw later in our trip, and actually have two cats named Bilbo and Frodo.

Therefore, we always allocate enough time for any *oopsies* or *what-ifs* that might occur. Sure, you can never plan for everything, but we try to make allowances for the most likely snags we could encounter. For traveling to Australia from the Midwest, there weren't a lot of appealing options for flights on a single carrier. So we ended up doing the domestic legs of our travel on Delta, to take advantage of frequent flyer miles, then transferred to their partner airline, Air New Zealand, and booked a separate ticket for the international portions of the journey.

For us, this resulted in the best combination of cost, comfort, and number of layovers. Believe it or not, Mr. Rylon doesn't like to fly. In order to get on a plane, he takes prescribed anti-anxiety medication and washes it down with a glass of wine or two. So when we travel, we try to minimize the number of take-offs (his least favorite part) and, therefore, connections.

With all that considered, we still ended up with a multi-carrier flight situation. Flights to Australia often depart the west coast of the United States late at night. Given the length of the flight, time changes, and crossing the International Date Line, this means you typically arrive on the morning two days after you set out, despite only 15 hours or so of real time passing while you're in the air. If you were to miss your flight, you'd likely have to wait a full day to catch the next one. To make sure we wouldn't screw up our Air New Zealand flight from LAX due to any small delays in our original Delta flight, we booked our first flight at the ass crack of dawn.

Therefore, we arrived in Los Angeles pretty damn early on Thursday, September 7, 2017. Instead of denting our butts in the super uncomfortable plastic bucket seats in the airport all day before sitting on the even more uncomfortable plane all night, we decided to make the most of the layover.

The cool thing about LAX is that it's equipped for worldwide travelers in any situation. Just outside of the airport is a row of hotels. You can get a day rate at many of them, which allows for check-in around 9 a.m. and check-out around dinnertime. Most of these include an airport shuttle, use of a pool, and Wi-Fi, in addition to a place to nap or shower.

Here are a few that offer this option with their current rates:

- Travelodge – $79.95; also includes continental breakfast on arrival

(www.travelodgelax.com/halfday_dayratedayuse.htm)
- FourPoints by Sheraton – $109 (www.fourpointslax.com/hotel-by-lax-airport)
- Hilton Los Angeles Airport – $129 (www3.hilton.com/en/hotels/california/hilton-los-angeles-airport-LAXAHHH/index.html)
- Westin Los Angeles Airport – Call for pricing and availability

We booked a room at the Hilton. It was steeper than I wanted, but their online booking process is easy and painless, and they had availability. When we arrived at LAX, we saw numerous shuttle buses for Travelodge advertising their day rate as well. Unfortunately, I couldn't find a way to book it online, and I dislike calling to make reservations, but that's just a personal preference. Reviews were overall positive for this service and I would consider it in the future.

We dropped off our baggage at the hotel, then opted for some fun in the California sun. We took an Uber to the Santa Monica Pier. Although it's less than ten miles from the airport to the beach, be prepared for gnarly LAX traffic, which made our ride take about 45 minutes and cost $22 each way. With that said, I think it's worth the time and expense as long as you have it to spare.

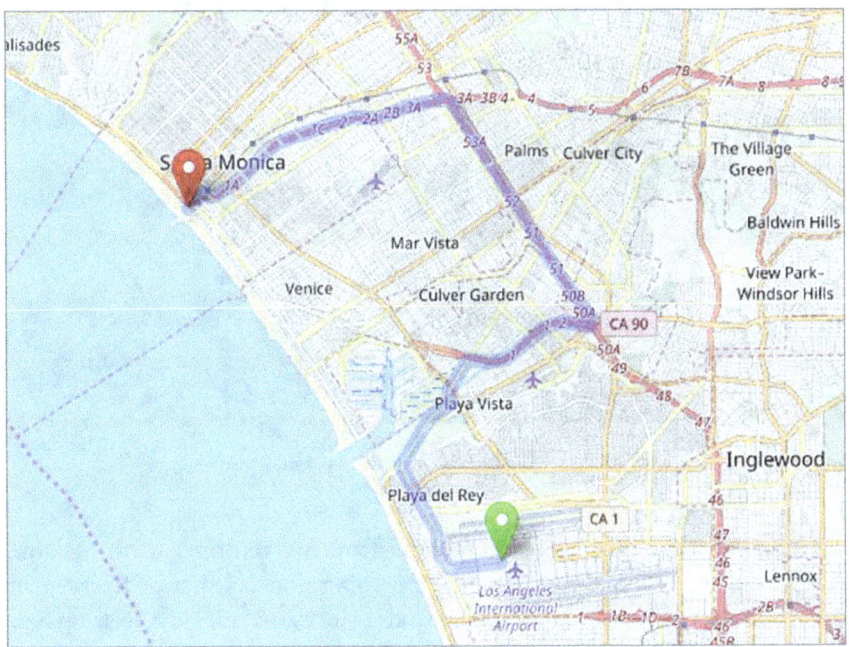

© OpenStreetMap contributors

Have your driver drop you at the street-level entrance to the pier and you can easily spend a few hours wandering down to the ocean and back. If you aren't up for a steep climb, ask to be let off at the boardwalk level instead, but I enjoy the views and additional eateries up top.

This was an amazing start to our vacation. Hanging out at the beach, grabbing lunch at one of the plentiful restaurants in the area, spotting some seals frolicking below the pier, people-watching, playing *Pokémon Go* at one of the most epic sites in the game (hey, 38-year-old ladies have to catch 'em all too, you know!)—any of it, *all* of it—are better options than counting the minutes back at the airport, in my opinion.

We spotted these motorcyclists enjoying the beautiful weather on our walk to the Santa Monica Pier.

After we'd had enough for one afternoon, we returned to the Hilton. Having the hotel room was worth it for one thing alone...a shower. It was great to be able to freshen up in a real bathroom since we'd already been up and traveling for nearly a full day by the time it was evening on the West Coast. It always helps to start rejuvenated when boarding a long flight.

Around that time, we started getting antsy about our upcoming departure. Remember, we're overly cautious! Although we probably had time to grab dinner somewhere near the hotel, we headed back to the airport. The international terminal actually has some pretty decent restaurants, so I don't feel like we missed out too much. I can highly recommend LuckyFish by Sushi Roku. They had great quality food, an awesome live band, and our meals were reasonably priced at under $20 per entree. If I'd had a shorter layover and was looking to kill some time at LAX, that would have been my pick for the entire stay.

Here's the moral of this story... We finished our meals with enough cushion for a leisurely stroll to our gate. But as we neared it, we realized something was wrong. Alarms kept going off everywhere. It was a system glitch, not a real emergency. However, this meant we—and people on every other international flight—had to walk what felt like five miles to some rarely used section of the terminal and then be bused to special freestanding ramps up to the jumbo jets.

The number of people we saw sprinting and nearly dying trying to make their flights made us pretty happy that we'd left plenty of time to spare in our schedule. At this point we felt like we'd already had a bit of adventure. Little did we know what was still to come...

DAY 2 – TRAVELING TO AUSTRALIA – GENERAL TIPS AND TRICKS

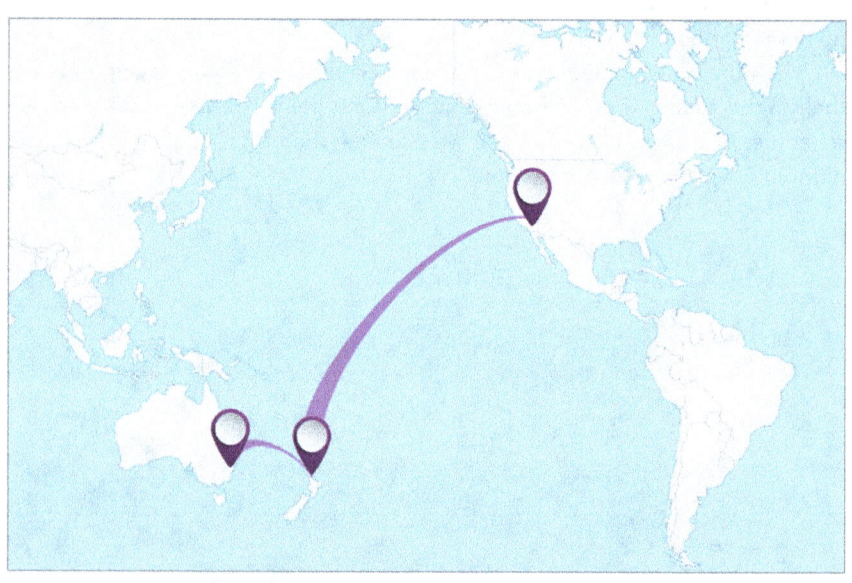

© OpenStreetMap contributors

Time for some real talk. When it comes to Australia and New Zealand trips, it's a pretty safe bet you're going to have to fly to get there unless you live on a sailboat or something, in which case I'd like to come visit and do a special edition of this guide based on my travels to see you!

No matter where you're leaving from, this is likely to be a doozy of a flight —both in terms of the length and cost. In fact, airfare accounted for nearly 45% of our total vacation spend. It's a great place to scrimp and save, except how comfortable you are on the trip plays a role in how much you can enjoy your destination on arrival.

Mr. Rylon and I aren't exactly built for tiny airline seats, if you know what I mean. Refer back to the introduction where I told you about how I spend most of my life in front of a computer, writing books. And did I mention that Mr. Rylon is terrified of flying? I admire him for conquering that fear every time we go somewhere by plane, but the less stress we put him through while in the air, the better.

Therefore, I searched high and low for the option that would provide the best compromise between cost and comfort. While business class lay-flat seats would be a dream come true, I wasn't about to fork over the cost of a brand-new car for one. No, seriously...they were going for more than $15,000 a piece last I looked. I'm going to need you all to buy a whole lot more of my novels to make that happen.

After consoling Mr. Rylon, I showed him a few other alternatives. Premium economy seats on international flights are really the equivalent of—or even better than—domestic first class in terms of seat width, leg room, meal options, and amenities. Still, those seats were running around $4,000-5,000 each.

To make things worse, economy classes on most of the long-haul flights have at least three seats to a section between the aisles. So when traveling as a couple, odds are good you'll cross the largest ocean on Earth getting to know someone else's life story or feeling awkward when they fall asleep on you or smelling their farts when they succumb mid-flight to gastrointestinal distress after choking down terrible airplane food.

What? Are my anti-social tendencies showing? Sorry. Ahem, back to business...

Mr. Rylon and I decided we might splurge and purchase a third seat between us so we would have some elbow room. I would recommend this if you're able to justify the cost. However, our favorite airline for this route is Air New Zealand. They have one other similar option that other carriers don't (to the best of my knowledge), and that's the one we went for.

It's called Skycouch. Now, don't get excited, because referring to this area as a couch is a heinous misrepresentation. Your home's super-cushy sectional won't magically appear midair. If you'd like to see the marketing hype for this class of service, check out the info and pictures here:

www.airnewzealand.co.uk/flights-to-california. For reality, see the image below.

Although it's not quite as sweet as you might imagine at first, Skycouch can still make a world of difference if you figure out how it works best for you.

Mr. Rylon enjoying a movie in the Skycouch leg of our Air Newzealand flight from LAX to Auckland.

Skycouch consists of three seats grouped together with other seats encroaching on your personal space in front of you like normal. This is still an economy class fare. You won't get any upgraded meal options or fancy amenity kits. However, you will get a row of three seats by a window for your party. If you're one, two, or three people, you get three seats for a single price. At the time I'm writing this, those three seats cost about the same as you'd pay buying 2.5 seats at the single-seat rate. To be exact, we paid $3,887.32 total for this fare, which included travel from LAX to Sydney via Auckland then a return trip from Auckland to LAX for both Mr. Rylon and me.

The one variation between standard economy seats and the Skycouch row seats are that the Skycouch has three independent footrests that lift up to make a solid lay-flat surface in your row. All armrests in the row (including the one closest to the side of the plane) fold up and give you room to use the entire space as you see fit.

A mass of bedding and pillows are also provided to make your nest as cozy as possible. The airline supplies you with a fluffy duvet to pad the seat, blankets, and pillows. Not those tiny suckers, either. These are legit pillows that you can use to prop yourself up against the wall or fill in gaps between the seats to make your area comfier.

Skycouch is advertised as "cuddle class". Images online would make you think you can spoon (but not fork!) with your travel companion comfortably within its confines. I think this is incredibly misleading unless you skip dessert a lot more than Mr. Rylon and I do. You'd also need to be vertically challenged to keep your feet fully inside your row while lying completely flat.

However, we did find some creative positions that kept us both from turning into human pretzels. The configuration that worked best for us was putting the middle seat and window seat foot rests up, turning that into an area that one of us could stretch out in while propped against the wall of the plane. Meanwhile, the other person reclined in the aisle seat, configured as normal. Sometimes the aisle passenger would tip over into the middle area, too. After the person had watched a movie or something for a while, we'd swap spots.

In this way, we were both able to get a decent amount of sleep on the flight, which lasted approximately fourteen hours. Unfortunately, Skycouch does nothing to block the sound of screaming kids, who understandably wanted off that plane five hours ago, in your immediate vicinity. All in all, I think it was worth the extra expense and made us comfortable enough that we were able to function and enjoy the day of our arrival in Sydney despite the seemingly endless voyage. Due to our long layover in California, and crossing the International Date Line, we left our house at first light on a Thursday but didn't finally step foot in Sydney until nearly noon on Saturday their time. Whew!

One final note: there are no direct flights from LAX to Sydney on Air New Zealand. You will be required to stop over and change planes in Auckland before continuing on. This wasn't a big deal since we got to stretch our legs for a bit. The airport in Auckland is small and the international transit process was painless. Besides, we were planning to travel to Auckland as we worked our way back to the US, so there was no inconvenience at all on the return journey.

Mr. Rylon and I, much happier after being upgraded to premium economy for the Auckland to Sydney leg of our trip.

Plus, we ended up getting upgraded to premium economy at minimal cost—through Air New Zealand's bidding system—for the final leg of our journey to Australia. To be perfectly honest, I still feel premium economy is a much better overall experience than Skycouch. The food is better, the seats were roomier, there were fewer people crammed into the space, and due to the increased recline and true footrests, it's easy to sleep there.

However, for under half the cost of premium economy when split by two passengers, Skycouch would still be my pick. I can deal with the downgrade for less than a day of my life. Your tolerance may vary, but if you save a bit here and can explore some more while actually at your destination, I think it's a fair tradeoff.

PART II

SYDNEY AND THE BLUE MOUNTAINS

DAY 3 – SYDNEY – BONDI BEACH

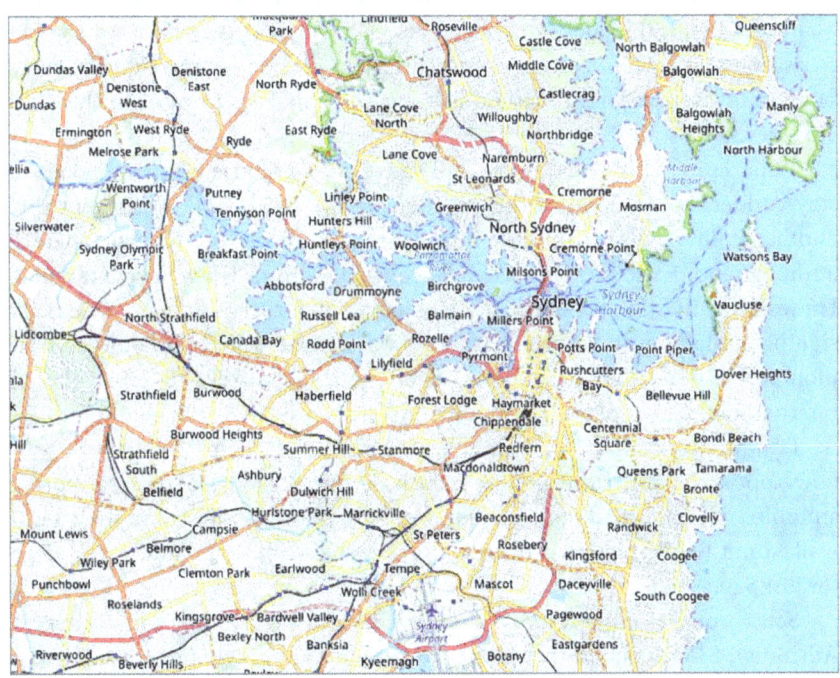

© OpenStreetMap contributors

Finally! We had arrived. Of course, there are some housekeeping things you need to attend to once you land. Slap yourself in the face a few times, try not to argue with your companion—who is likely to be at least as grouchy as you are due to sleep deprivation and enduring discomfort for nearly an entire day—make your way through immigration, collect your luggage, and *finally* pass customs.

If you're flying into Sydney as your original entry point into Australia, you have a few opportunities for conveniences that will make your trip easier if you don't blast right out of the airport on the other side of that mammoth flight. Believe me, I was eager to get the hell out of there, too, but I'm so glad we stopped at one particular kiosk.

No, not the currency exchange booth. That place is such a rip-off it makes me angry just seeing it! Friendly tip: withdraw money from ATMs instead of succumbing to the allure of the currency exchange booth. The fee will be much lower, in direct contrast to the usury rates at the place in or near airports and other tourist destinations. Also, some credit cards—including the platinum Delta Skymiles American Express, which I use—have no foreign transaction fees. So unless you're desperate, just say no to the foreign exchange booth and use a different method to get cash or make purchases in the local currency.

What I'm talking about, of course, is internet. Because everyone needs to stay connected when you're on vacation, right? Okay, well, that's probably another point of debate. Believe it or not, as the owner of my own romance author brand, I need to check emails constantly. Even when we're traveling, I'm working. In this case, the primary objective of our trip was to attend a book signing in Melbourne, so...yeah...internet was a must. Besides, if I don't call my mom on the regular, or at least email her, she's likely to send out an international search party. (Hi, Mom!)

I've rarely seen an operation as efficient and helpful as the Optus (www.optus.com.au) store in the arrivals terminal of the Sydney airport. I stumbled in, half dead, and handed over my phone. A few minutes later, I walked out (while texting my mom, of course) all connected and ready to go for just $40.58.

Some considerations...make sure you have a phone that can accept an Australian SIM card and that it's not tethered to any single provider. I used a Samsung Galaxy S8 that I bought unlocked at Best Buy, and it has worked flawlessly every time I've traveled outside of the US with it.

My SIM card purchase got me unlimited local calls and texts, a crap ton of data (20GB), and an international allowance. All of these were valid for a period of 30 days. Also, once you have the SIM card, you can top it up from an app on your phone if you run out. Honestly, I didn't come close to consuming my allotment even with my constant email checking, using my phone for GPS on our day trips, uploading photos to Instagram and Facebook, and turning my phone into a hot spot so that Mr. Rylon could browse the internet when I was ignoring him to do work during our meals and train rides, etc. Oops.

After we took care of that, we were finally, FINALLY, going to leave the airport and see koalas and kangaroos hopping past while eating Vegemite and waving the Australian flag. Okay, not really, but that's sort of how my delusional, sleep-deprived brain imagined it.

From the airport, we took a cab because it was painless. They were lined up right there as we exited the building. However, the Uber network in both Sydney and Melbourne is robust if you prefer that. The ride took about a half an hour and cost $35.26. There is also a train called AirportLink (www.airportlink.com.au) that will get you from the airport to the city itself. It was going to be $16 per person and more hassle than I felt like dealing with at that moment, considering we were hauling around suitcases jammed full of books. I'm not quite forty yet, but sometimes I turn to Mr. Rylon and proclaim, "I'm too old for that! Let's just do it the easy way."

This was one of those times.

By now you might be wondering where the heck you're going to stay. My recommendation is that you don't opt for a hotel. Sure, they're easy and generally a safe bet. In my opinion, they're also extremely overpriced, especially in a major city center. I prefer to rent an apartment from a private owner that has more amenities for a lower cost.

Lately, Airbnb has become the most popular service for connecting homeowners and travelers. I've also used VRBO in the past. On this trip, we rented an apartment through Airbnb in both Sydney and Melbourne. I couldn't have been happier with that choice.

Some perks of renting an apartment include saving money on certain meals so you can splurge on others. Personally, I'm not a big fan of breakfast. I'm perfectly content to pick up some groceries to make Mr. Rylon (who is both diabetic and also a breakfast-lover—how are we even married?) scrambled eggs with a side of some sort of breakfast meat, and eat something quick like a bowl of cereal or some fruit myself. Besides, visiting a grocery store in a foreign country is one of my favorite things to do. Trying food you've never seen before and seeing how people eat day to day in a foreign place is fun, interesting, and informative.

Another benefit on a long trip is that most Airbnbs will have laundry facilities either in the apartment or in the building. This greatly helps reduce how much you have to pack.

Some of the apartments for rent will be in neighborhoods that give you a better feel for the city than the downtown tourist options. In this case, we opted to stay in Potts Point. The restaurants and shops surrounding our apartment were phenomenal. I think if we'd only stayed downtown in Sydney, I would have a much different perspective on the city and what life is really like for the people who live in and around it.

Therefore, I can personally recommend Helen's flat. Here's her Airbnb listing: www.airbnb.com/rooms/7485131. She was incredibly responsive to my questions, made sure we had everything we needed, and her apartment was fully stocked—from kitchen utensils to guidebooks, and even Opal cards, which are used to pay for public transportation—to make our trip amazing. The only slight downside is that it is on the third floor with no elevator. Carrying our luggage (full of books for my book signings, remember?) up the stairs was a bit of a hassle. However, it was only on arrival and departure that it was inconvenient. The other times, the walk up didn't bother us much. If we can do it—refer back to my sedentary life as an author—then unless you have a physical limitation that would necessitate a ground-floor apartment, I think it's well worth it.

If you haven't used Airbnb yet, they gave me this link to share: http://www.airbnb.com/c/loryna11. This means that if you use it to set up your account, you get a $55 travel credit. Full disclosure, if you then go on a trip, they give me a $20 toward a future stay also. Fun for everyone! Woohoo!

Our flight arrived around 10 a.m. By the time we got to the apartment and settled in for a few minutes, it was close to noon. Plenty of time left in the day to get out there and begin to get acclimated to the city.

Much to Mr. Rylon's chagrin, Vacation Boot Camp had officially begun!

Okay, not exactly. What we did was buy a pass to the hop-on-hop-off bus. Sure, they're a little bit cheesy, but fun. I tend to like these tours (except in megacities like NY or London where traffic can reduce their usefulness) because they take you to all the highlights. After making a circuit and hearing about the stops through the onboard narration, you can choose which you prefer to explore in greater depth. You'll cover a lot of ground, hit all the important stops, and be treated to commentary about the sights as you pass by so you actually know what it is you're seeing and the significance of it. In our case, we thought it might be a nice way to sit down and get an overview of Sydney while fighting jet lag.

There are two major brands of hop-on-hop-off bus chains that I've used from Spain, to China, to Australia. Big Bus Tours (www.bigbustours.com/en/sydney/sydney-bus-tours) and City Sightseeing (city-sightseeing.com) are the major players. They're pretty comparable, both offering 24-hour access (with an option to extend your ticket to 48 hours if you like), free Wi-Fi on the bus, headphones, maps, and even rain ponchos. Both are double decker buses with open tops. The routes can be slightly different in each city, so check their websites and see which one fits your goals best or go with whichever you happen to walk past first!

From Potts Point, we only had to walk down five or six blocks to get to a stop on the blue line of the Big Bus, which would take us out to world-famous Bondi Beach. There is also a red line on the Big Bus in Sydney, which is the standard city tour. Each route takes approximately 90 minutes if you stay on the bus and make a full circuit. The buses come about every 20 minutes between 8:30 a.m. and 5 p.m., so you should never have too long of a wait either to start your trip or to resume it if you hop off somewhere that catches your eye. Since we bought our tickets in the afternoon, we also had the option to use them for the city tour the next morning if we chose. Plan your timing wisely to get the most bang for your buck.

You can pay onboard either of the buses. They also offer discounts if you buy your tickets in advance. If you purchase in advance, the bus costs $35.73 for twenty-four hours or $48.72 for forty-eight hours. Otherwise, you can grab a ticket onboard for $39.70 or $54.14 respectively.

Be sure to read the offer details, though, because for some of them you have to have your ticket printed out and in hand, not just on your phone. When you're somewhere without easy access to a printer, that could be a pain.

And we were off!

Sydney is a spectacular city located on the southeast coast of Australia. It's the capital of its state—New South Wales—but not the country itself, as many people believe. That honor belongs to Canberra, which lies about 175 miles southwest of Sydney.

The city straddles the bay, and the Harbour Bridge spanning it—connecting the two halves—is one of the greatest landmarks in the world along with the iconic Opera House, perched beneath it. There is a lot of green space to complement the sea views, most notably Hyde Park and the Royal Botanical Gardens. At the heart of all this is Circle Quay, a transportation hub for ferries and cruises as well as a tourism center. As you venture outward from the bay itself, you will gradually climb up low-lying hills. If you were to continue a few hours west of Sydney, those hills would become the Blue Mountains. I'll tell you more about that a few days further in our itinerary.

One of the things I should have expected but was surprised by, given my mental image of Australia from an American perspective, was the rich Asian influence. In the people and food, including but not limited to an entire Chinatown neighborhood, Asian cultures were prominently represented.

We rode the bus most of the loop around, checking out the city and outlying neighborhoods, before disembarking at Bondi Beach.

It was September when we visited, which is early spring for Sydney. It was both chilly, with a high in the low sixties, and windy. Though it wasn't bikini weather, Bondi Beach will always make for an impressive landscape. A wide stretch of sand in the middle is flanked by hills on each end. The beach meets the ocean, which was roaring in when we visited. Caution when swimming there is advised, with one end of the beach being subject to an infamous rip current.

Another highlight of this area is the Bondi Baths (icebergs.com.au). This is a public pool that has been an attraction for more than 100 years. It is perched right on the edge of the ocean, with seawater pouring over the edge when there are high tides or strong waves. Admission is $7 for adults or $5 for children, including the pools and sauna, and it is open all year round.

An impressive whale shark kite flies over Bondi Beach.

While we didn't get to go in the water, we got to experience something equally fun. All up and down the beach, people were flying giant kites, including one spectacular giant shaped like a whale shark. Those are one of our favorite animals as we love to SCUBA dive and were fortunate enough to dive with whale sharks in the Georgia Aquarium once, but that's another guide!

To warm up after wandering the beach and peeking at the Baths, we ducked into Lush (www.facebook.com/LushOnBondi), which is a very reasonably priced café. It also has heat lamps on the porch tables should you happen to visit on a similar day. We tried the sweet potato wedges. They were super cool because they came with disposable ketchup dispensers that we'd never seen before. For our snacks, a coffee, and a pot of hot tea, we paid less than ten dollars. Plus you can't beat the view.

Once we'd finished and hung around a few minutes to be closer to the time the bus would be back, we wandered along some of the many shops—featuring everything from souvenirs to active wear—lining Gould Street until our ride arrived. We rode the bus back toward Potts Point, electing to hop off a stop before our own in order to take advantage of the butchers and farm markets near the Edgecliff station and stock up our fridge.

There is also a chain of standard supermarkets called Woolworths (www.woolworths.com.au), if you're looking for something less adventurous and reliable for prepackaged goods. For those of you wondering, no, the stores are no relation to the five and dime stores we used to have in the US. The one in Potts Point had all the essentials and was open from 7 a.m. until midnight every day. In most places outside of the United States, plastic bag usage is minimized. Be prepared to pay a small fee for bags or bring your own when shopping.

In total we spent $35.26 on groceries, which lasted us for all three days we were in Sydney. We cooked our own breakfasts and ate some lunches and snacks from that as well as having drinks to carry around with us during our day trips.

Even though we took the chance to stock up, neither of us felt like cooking that night considering we were all discombobulated from hardly having slept and crossing the world's largest ocean—including the International Date Line—earlier that day. That wasn't an issue as there are plenty of restaurants in the Potts Point area.

We opted to pick something up on the way home, while wandering through our temporary neighborhood. I tend to use Tripadvisor to select places to try, and the reviews for Fei Jai (https://feijai.com/) were phenomenal, with good reason. We ate here two or three times during our stay in Sydney, and loved everything we tried. Two people can eat well for under $50, including a couple of drinks. We'd highly recommend trying it, especially the prawn and chive gow gee!

DAY 4 – SYDNEY – FEATHERDALE, OPERA HOUSE, AND THE FARMHOUSE

The time change coming from the US to Australia is a lot for your body to adjust to. I think for our entire trip, we were in bed and asleep by nine or ten most nights. After forcing ourselves to stay awake the day before, we had a solid night's sleep and were ready to hit the ground running the next morning on our first full day in Australia.

So we decided to take public transportation out to a suburb of Sydney to do the quintessential Australian thing...get our picture taken with a koala! Okay, I know, it sounds horribly cheesy and possibly irresponsible if the animals are exploited for tourism. However, I was willing to give it a go because I did a lot of research on the conditions at our destination. The koalas aren't held by each person. They're left to sleep or do whatever koalas do in a low branch where you can come up and pet them. This is less stressful for the animals. Plus, my mom's favorite animals are koalas and she's afraid of flying, so a picture of me with a cute gray koala was about as close as she is ever going to get to experiencing this for herself.

I'm so glad we went to Featherdale Wildlife Park (www.featherdale.com.au). It was a far better experience than I'd imagined. First, because of how we got there. We took an Uber to the train station. Remember how I mentioned their network is robust? It's an easy way to get around. We took about ten rides in our three days in Sydney with an average cost of about $10 each time.

For the longer stretch of our journey, we opted to take the train rather than rent a car and fight with traffic or pay for an Uber the whole way from the city center to the park. Although it's only 30 miles away, it would be about an hour drive. Plus, it's always an adventure to figure out public transportation in a new city.

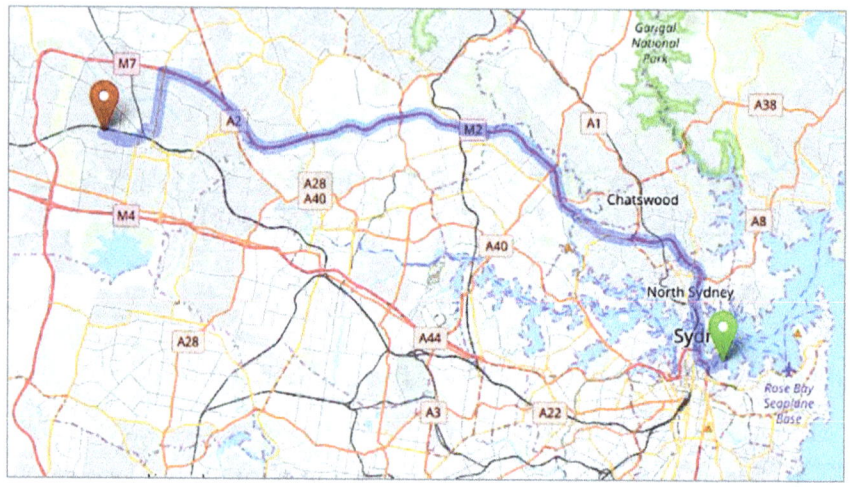

© OpenStreetMap contributors

To be honest, we struggled a bit with figuring out the local system. Although there was a sign that said you had to tap in with your Opal Card (www.opal.com.au/en/about-opal/opal_for_visitors), we found you could actually skip past that into the station. Once inside, head to the information desk in order to buy and activate a card that will allow you to access the trains, buses, and ferries throughout the city. We bought each of us a card with enough funds for a few days. Twenty dollars should do you unless you plan to use public transportation exclusively to get around. As a bonus, on Sundays a single fare of $1.95 will cover you all day no matter how many trips or transfers you make.

Remember too that our Airbnb—and probably many others—had these cards available in our apartment. We left ours behind with the residual balance on them for the next guests. So be sure to check around before you head out for the first time. It's easier to top up a card than get a new one, and if you're cutting it close on a departure time, it could save you from having to wait for the next train.

From the central station, we rode the light rail on the North Shore and Western line for about an hour. It was a great way to see several neighborhoods and get a feel for the sprawling Sydney suburbs, which seemed inviting, clean, and overall not that different from ours back home. It also makes me jealous of the public transportation systems in many foreign countries. I wish we had more options like theirs.

Once we reached Blacktown Station, we were told we could transfer to a bus from Stand E for a short ten-minute ride to the park. Again, this would be the most cost-effective way to finish the trip. However, when we looked at the schedule posted on the stop, we realized it was going to take over an hour for the next bus to arrive. It felt like a long wait for a short ride, so we left the train station and called another trusty Uber. A ride from the train station to the park was $9. Considering we only had so much time to visit the country, the cost of wasting some of it is also a factor to me, so I don't mind paying to get somewhere quicker sometimes.

As for the park itself, it far exceeded my expectations. It cost $17 per person for admission, plus we opted to get a cup of kangaroo food and a paid-for the picture with a koala for my mom, which was an additional $18 (up to four people included in the up-close encounter for a single fee).

Once inside, I realized that this was a better setup than a typical zoo. In the wallaby section, for example, the animals were allowed to roam freely. The walkways are lined with a single rail fence at about knee height. The wallabies can easily go under when they don't want to be bothered by people. On the other hand, they are welcome to come out and mingle or eat some food from your little plastic cup whenever they choose.

This wallaby hopped out from under the wooden barrier behind him to visit with us and eat some of the food we offered it.

It was really great to be in and among the animals, who seemed very relaxed and happy. We had a lot of fun observing them, even spotting a mother carrying her baby in her pouch. It was a very peaceful place, with a lot of benches to stop and sit and listen to what seemed like millions of birds around us. The park is filled with more species of birds than I knew existed. We had a really enjoyable time wandering around, taking pictures of the bright colors and species that are so different from animals we know from home.

All in all, we'd only planned to stay here for three or four hours. If you went with children or really enjoy these types of things, I'd budget a full day. There is a café on premises and water fountains throughout the sanctuary, so it would be easy to stay longer.

Mr. Rylon and I wandered around for most of the morning, then headed out close to lunchtime. We rode the train back to Sydney, and used the hop-on-hop-off bus to head toward the Opera House (www.sydneyoperahouse.com). While en route, I booked tickets for a tour of the famous landmark on my phone. We hadn't done that ahead of time because we were waffling about how we'd feel and if it would be too hectic. I'm thankful we went ahead with the visit as it turned out to be a highlight of our stay.

Tours run from 9 a.m. to 5 p.m. every day, departing every 15 or 30 minutes. They cost $29 per person, and last for an hour.The history and significance of the opera house make for an incredible story, one I'm sure I wouldn't have fully understood if I'd simply gone and walked around the outside of the building to admire its architecture. The structure is impressive, unique, and gorgeous. It juts out into the Sydney Harbour and is surrounded by water on three sides. The reflections of the blazing Sydney sun make it gleam. However, the information we learned, and the areas we were able to visit that are inaccessible to the public otherwise, definitely enhanced my experience and my appreciation of this landmark.

I also enjoyed that the tour guides here use a sound system to augment their narration. Everyone wears headphones and the guide has a microphone, so we were able to hear clearly even when our group spread out or went outside, where it was windy.

I'll leave the really good stuff for you to discover there on your own. Suffice it to say that the story behind the opera house is riddled with politics, drama, and betrayal. It would make a decent plot for one of the shows performed inside it, including a tragic ending for Jørn Utzon, the man who designed the iconic structure yet never saw it with his own eyes after it had been completed, despite the fact that he lived to be 90 years old and only passed away in 2008, when the Opera House was already celebrating its 35th anniversary.

Here's a fun fact to balance out that sad trivia tidbit: the stages have no wings to wait in! The unconventional design of the opera house means all sets have to be lifted into place from above or below and not slid in from the side. The set storage room, located 33 feet below the stage, is featured in the tour.

The view from the entrance to the concert hall is every bit as stunning as the performances themselves.

The components used in the construction of the building alone are worth taking a peek at. Mr. Rylon is a woodworker. He pointed out that the wood of the concert hall is a gorgeous mix of white birch and Australian brush box. In addition to looking beautiful, the materials and shape make the concert hall world-renowned for its acoustic properties. We got to hear a snippet from a rehearsal for a performance and it did sound incredible, both warm and clear.

Even the roof tiles are interesting. They were made in Sweden and contain clay and stone. Some are glossy and some are matte. There are more than a million of them set in a chevron pattern on the sail-like structures of the opera house roof. American architect Louis Kahn once wrote, "The sun did not know how beautiful its light was, until it was reflected off this building."

There aren't any supports in the foyers outside the main opera house and concert hall or in the theaters themselves to obstruct the views of the performances or the harbor and bridge. Standing there, looking out at the water and the boats passing by through the massive curved glass walls, is like watching another show.

One note…at the time of this publication, the entire opera house is not accessible to people who are unable to climb stairs. It is under renovation with the goal of making the main stages more accessible. Currently there is no elevator, and attending a performance in the opera theater or the concert hall requires a climb of about four or five stories each. The same goes for the tour.

Now, on the other hand, if you *really* like stairs, you should go for the Sydney Harbour Bridge Climb (www.bridgeclimb.com). Yes, you can walk across the bridge the traditional way, at road level. But you can also conquer the peak of the arch above the bridge if you can tackle the 1,332 steps and four ladders standing between you and the top. I can only assume the views are spectacular as there was no way I was about to clamber up there to find out.

Now, something I'm much better suited for: eating! There are several options at the opera house, most notably an extremely fancy restaurant called Bennelong (www.bennelong.com.au) that grants a gorgeous view of the harbor bridge and the skyline. Be sure to make reservations well in advance, dress up if you brought appropriate formalwear, and be prepared to shell out about $250 for two people if you care to dine there.

Mr. Rylon and I opted to try a different sort of experience. During my research for the trip, I had read about a restaurant called The Farmhouse (www.farmhousekingscross.com.au), located not too far from our Airbnb in Kings Cross. Though it wasn't at the time, it is right now ranked number one out of nearly five thousand restaurants in Sydney! I can tell you it has earned that designation.

What I didn't realize when I messaged their team, which consists of just six people, about a reservation is that it's a very intimate place with ONE table. Everyone eats together—the same meal at the same time. You will have neighbors you don't know when you start out, but you are likely to leave with new friends along with a very happy belly. It is open Wednesday through Sunday and has two sittings each night. The menu consists of five courses determined by the chef with no substitutions, although they do accommodate dietary restrictions if you notify them in advance.

Don't worry, everything is absolutely delicious. It was a mix of flavors and offerings with a rustic home-style feel despite the fancy ingredients in some of the dishes. I can't imagine even a picky eater would leave hungry here; there was something for everyone and the portions were beyond generous.

After having my heart set on the place, I was disappointed when they wrote back and let me know they were full. However, I explained we were coming from across the world and only in town for a few days. They said they'd let me know if they had any cancellations, and were good enough to do just that.

Dinner at Farmhouse was one of the most extraordinary meals I've ever had, and Mr. Rylon and I pride ourselves on being foodies. Not only for the to-die-for courses—from the blue swimmer crab with asparagus, cashew, and roe to the beef cheek and mushrooms, and of course the baked pear tart for dessert—but also for the ambiance and the experience as well.

Seriously, though, the food alone would be worth it.

Rustic, home-style food with flair combine with the atmosphere and an amazing staff to make The Farmhouse top notch.

Another thing I loved was that they truly make the most of a tiny space. The kitchen was open, so you could watch the meal being prepared while our servers changed out the mismatched plates, and kept us company, in between courses. I felt like a guest at someone's house rather than a customer at an exclusive restaurant.

Did I mention that the entire meal was only $43.30 per person? Yup. I would gladly have paid three times that and still felt like I'd gotten more than my money's worth.

I only wish we could have eaten here more than once during our trip. I absolutely recommend that you try it. Don't be like me, though. You do not want to take the chance of missing out on this one. Book well in advance!

DAY 5 – BLUE MOUNTAINS – SCENIC WORLD AND JENOLAN CAVES

© OpenStreetMap contributors

After checking out all the options for activities in and around Sydney, I knew I wanted to organize a day trip outside of the city. In fact, if we're staying three or more days in any given destination, which is kind of our comfortable minimum to reduce the hassle of packing and unpacking too frequently, we like to do this in most places.

Based on the days we had available and the timing of organized tours of the surrounding areas that left from the city, none of the companies were able to meet our needs. Therefore, we decided to rent a car and venture to the Blue Mountains on our own. Bayswater Car Rental (www.bayswatercarrental.com.au) made it easy (and affordable) to do so. A compact car for the day cost us $98.17.

Pick-up was from the intersection of William and Dowling Streets starting at 7 a.m., a full hour before any of the other international rental companies I investigated. Their facility was large, bright, clean, and a well-oiled machine. We were in, doing our paperwork, then driving away before we knew it.

Now, one thing to consider is how comfortable you are driving in one of the world's mega metropolises. Especially one as hectic as Sydney. The tangle of one-way streets in the downtown area seemed to confuse even some of our local Uber drivers, who do this for a living. On top of that, there is a *lot* of traffic. We had intended to cross the Harbour Bridge and leave that way, but got turned around and settled for a more southerly route that took us past the airport instead.

I believe there was more congestion in this direction, especially during the main morning commute. The reality is that all routes in and out will be packed at peak hours. So if you're going to do this day trip, consider the timing and direction of traffic. If you're a more timid driver than Mr. Rylon, who missed his calling as a world rally driver, then you might want to give it a while for things to settle down before embarking.

In fact, if your traveling companion doesn't like to zoom down the highway with white knuckles and their eyes half closed, maybe you should take pity on them. I might have left some permanent dents in the door handle of our poor little rental.

Oh yeah, and if you're from most other places in the world…

Rylon Recommendation **Remember to drive on the wrong side of the road!**

It was a bit of a journey, but a nice one, through rolling hills that gradually developed into mountains. The road was lined with long, pale grass, which probably gets pretty charred in summer, along with a smattering of trees with thin, gnarled trunks. As the elevation grew, so did the density of the woodland surrounding us, until we were engulfed in greenery interrupted only by small towns along the way.

Although it's only about sixty-seven miles from the car rental location to our first stop, Scenic World (www.scenicworld.com.au), it took approximately two hours to reach Katoomba, the town it's in. Scenic World is a bit touristy, but still worth a visit. After all, you are a tourist! Entry fees are $28.16 per person and get you access for the full day, though unless you like to hike, I don't think you will spend that much time here. It's open every day from 9 a.m. to 5 p.m., so if you leave Sydney around 7 a.m. you'll roll up just in time for opening and miss a lot of the crowds. This is part of what helped us enjoy what we wanted with short lines before moving on to our next adventure.

Scenic World is an outdoor park with four main means of transportation they call their "ways". These are also a large part of the attraction. For the price of admission, you can try them all out as many times as you like while taking in a glorious view of the Three Sisters. This is an unusual rock formation of three spires, each of which are over three thousand feet tall. Aboriginal lore says they were three sisters—Meehni, Wimlah, and Gunnedoowho—who were turned to stone by a witchdoctor in order to protect them during a war that broke out when they fell in love with forbidden men from a neighboring tribe. Unfortunately, the witchdoctor was killed in the conflict and, therefore, the sisters were not able to be released from their craggy forms.

As a romance author, I tend to enjoy stories like these. You never know where the next inspiration for one of my novels will come from! Even if that's not your thing, the formations themselves and the valley surrounding them make for a spectacular view. There are even a few waterfalls around, the most impressive of which is Katoomba Falls. You can both see and access the falls from Scenic World.

Mr. Rylon looks across a piece of the Jamison valley toward the main building of Scenic World, perched on the opposite cliff.

So what are those four methods of getting around I mentioned? The cableway, the railway, the walkway, and the skyway. The entry to Scenic World is at the top of a giant cliff; however, most of the incredible walking paths are down on the Jamison Valley floor. This includes 2.4 kilometers of smooth, elevated wooden boardwalk—the walkway—that makes wandering through the forest comfortable for people of all physical ability levels and reduces the impact of millions of visitors a year on the environment. It is lined with benches, and designed so that there are possible paths ranging from a ten-minute stroll to a full hour walk.

Instead of making you rappel down, or even worse, take a bazillion stairs, to get to the valley floor, Scenic World has come up with a couple of great solutions that make the most of this incredible landscape.

My favorite is the funicular, which is the steepest incline railway in the world with a 128% incline. It was originally used to haul coal from the mines below. Several statues, exhibits, and signs along the walkway explain the importance of the industry to the region. They also depict how the coal was removed from the mountains. You can even peek into one of the mine entrances. Never before has it been so fun to pretend you were a lump of coal as when you're speeding up or down the incline railway!

These days, a bright red train with glass walls and ceilings runs on the tracks. It gets a little difficult to tell what exactly is part of the ceiling and what is the wall because the seats swivel. As you board and take your seat, you appear to be reclining, staring at the glass ceiling. But once you leave the station, there are points where you're nearly vertical and kneeling on the rests to look out that same panel, which is now more like the wall. The people who were in the rows in front and in back of you are now above and below you.

It is both a thrilling ride (though not too scary for children or too intense for older guests) and another unique vantage point to take in the incredible surroundings. The brief tunnel section of the trip made me feel a little like Indiana Jones in the Temple of Doom. Fortunately, we all made it down safely, despite the screams of one rider who enjoyed the experience less than Mr. Rylon and me.

If that sounds like a little much for you, there is another, more sedate option. The cableway makes the same trek from the clifftop to the valley floor and back to the top. You can ride either, both, or one each way if you like. I'm not going to lie, Mr. Rylon and I loved the incline railway so much we rode it three times. However, we still tried out the cableway as well.

What is it? It's essentially a glass box dangling from angled steel cables by a giant metal arm. It can hold up to 84 passengers at a time. Inside, stair-stepped platforms ensure everyone has a perfect view of the Three Sisters and Katoomba Falls as you're floating through the canopy of trees that look like they came from the time of dinosaurs. It is slow moving and gentle as it lowers you over the course of its 1800-foot length.

So what's the last transportation method at Scenic World for? The skyway acts as a mobile bridge between the two outposts on top of the cliffs on either side of the ravine. It's strung between the entrance to Scenic World and the ridge that the Three Sisters are a part of.

It's similar to the cableway except it's level instead of on an incline, and when you reach the center you're suspended 900 feet above the valley floor. The good news is that there are panoramic views of the rock formations, the forest, the mountains, and the falls.

Did I mention that it also has a strip of glass flooring down the center in case you'd like to get a very good feel for exactly how much air there is between you and the ground far, far, *far* below you? This is definitely not an activity for someone who's afraid of heights. Everyone else...all aboard.

The east station is where you'll want to disembark if you're interested in doing some more serious hiking. Maps you can pick up at the stations show trails leading to Echo Point and beyond.

Once you've exhausted all the various "ways" and have taken a tour of the rainforest below, you'll probably end up heading back to the main building around lunchtime. Normally I would avoid a café in a tourist attraction in favor of just about any other food. It's generally overpriced, uninventive, bland, and of poor quality.

That is not the case with the Scenic World terrace café. In fact, the best basket of fish and chips I've ever had came from this place. It was fresh, with a light and crispy tempura coating. I learned later that they try to use locally sourced, high-quality ingredients in their offerings. My tastebuds could tell!

They also have a more formal, relatively speaking, sit down option called Eats270 (because it's 270 meters above the Jamison Valley floor). Though the restaurant offerings also looked great, we opted for the grab-and-go style café because we didn't want to take too much time with lunch when we had a lot more on our schedule for the day. From Katoomba we were heading farther west in a very indirect and squiggly route.

The next stop, Jenolan Caves (www.jenolancaves.org.au). This massive network of subterranean fun is located just twelve or thirteen miles from Scenic World as the crow flies. Too bad I can't fly.

ATTENTION – TWISTY, NARROW ROAD ALERT!!!

By car, it is about fifty miles of squirmy, squiggly driving between Scenic World and Jenolan Caves. Now would be a good time to pop some Dramamine if you ever get the hint of car sickness on normal routes. Don't let that scare you off, though. It is absolutely worth going to Jenolan. But be prepared.

In addition to being curvy, the road progressively narrows. It is steep, with little shoulder. There is a drastic drop off just beyond the guard rail at points. Plus, we passed plenty of wombat and kangaroo crossing signs. These are great for a funny picture, but also serious. We saw plenty of carcasses to prove that the danger of hitting one of these animals is real. I wouldn't want to be stuck out there with a damaged car at night. So plan accordingly!

Speaking of that, when tour buses come the opposite direction, leaving the caves, you could have to stop or even back up to give way. To cause less trouble, the road is closed to traffic leaving Jenolan from 11:45 a.m. to 1:15 p.m. every day, effectively making it a one-way road during those times. This is because tours arrive at those times. Knowing that, you might want to schedule your tours before the influx of visitors.

To be honest, there weren't many people there the day we visited and it wasn't an issue. I could see it being flooded during holidays or in peak travel season. For good reason!

The Jenolan caves were one of my favorite things we saw in Australia. In fact, I wish we'd had an extra day to spend here. If you can swing it, stay overnight at the cave campus so you can explore the area more completely. It's picturesque, nestled in the valley where the cave system begins.

As you approach, you drive through a massive stone archway so thick it's nearly a tunnel. On the other side, the Tudor chalets make it seem as if you've been transported to another time and place. Somewhere cozy that you might like to curl up and read for a while before tromping around underground, or to come back to once your legs are worn out from all that climbing.

Because it is a bit of a drive from anywhere, a tour or two at the caves gives you time to stretch your legs as much as you like before heading back. While you can certainly make this trip in a single day—we did—it would be more comfortable if you split it into two. But, hey, this isn't Vacation Boot Camp for nothing, right?

Although you might have your trusty SIM card from the airport, it will most likely struggle to work at Jenolan Caves. Rock on all sides, out in the middle of nowhere—you get the point.

Rylon Reccomendation Therefore, if you have any ticket confirmations or maps that you might need when you're down there, it's best to take a screen capture of them before you leave Scenic World. In fact, I do this with almost every confirmation email or digital ticket I get when going on a trip like this. It's better to have it stored in my phone's image gallery than to rely on the internet.

Here's another *really* helpful hint. When you go to the caves, there are about twenty different tours you can take. You should absolutely not pick blindly based on a time you think will fit in your schedule. There is a helpful list both online and on a wooden board at the cave entrance that lists the number of stairs on each tour. Pay attention unless you want to die!

No, seriously. Some of the tours have more than 1500 steps, and a couple even have vertical ladders. Others have more than 500 stairs you need to climb on the outside before you even reach the entrance to those particular caves. While those tours admittedly sounded amazing, I wouldn't know because there's no way in hell Mr. Rylon was going to agree to that even if I could force myself to attempt it. He does draw the line somewhere. Somewhere around 2000 stairs is apparently that spot.

Fortunately, there are also plenty of options that only require moderate exertion. You need to be able to climb stairs, but not a ton of them. The ones you'll have to scale are even and nicely spaced out. For example, we did the Imperial Cave tour, which follows the bed of an ancient river. So it is mostly smooth and flat except for an optional excursion down 66 stairs hewn out of the rock that takes you down to the current level of the ancient river.

I'm not going to lie, that was a tight, twisty, uneven 66 stairs each way. Still, we were rewarded for braving them. The water down at the bottom is so still and clear that you almost can't see it at first, until your eyes adjust. Then it takes on an otherworldly aqua glow. From down there you get a great view of an old shaft people used to spelunk (I've always wanted to use that word in a book, people!) into the cave before there were nice stairs and handrails and lights for us wimpy folks.

It was a one-hour tour with 358 total steps. Spread out over that time, it was not at all strenuous. The formations inside the cave were amazing from wide, blunt pillars to sharp white stalactites jabbing down from the ceiling to mineral deposits that looked almost like bacon hanging on the wall.

Interesting formations inside the Imperial Cave. This one reminds me of bacon!

The most famous cave at Jenolan is the Lucas Cave. It holds the broken pillar formation as well as the cathedral, which is the highest chamber in the system at 177 feet tall. It's often used for weddings and even concerts! This is one of the caves that requires you climb 252 stairs to reach the entrance and has another 658 stairs inside, but there are benches for resting along the way. The tour lasts for 90 minutes.

Having done a single tour here, I could see taking another two or three without getting the slightest bit bored. Unfortunately, we had to keep moving. Not without one last treat, though.

The most unexpected perk of our trip to Jenolan caves was finding out that the neon blue lake (tinted by the limestone in the rock) just beyond the cave entrances is home to several platypuses! Who doesn't want to see those? I mean, after koalas and kangaroos and wombats and Vegemite, they have to be quite possibly the most Australian thing ever, right?

The Blue Lake is home to a family of platypuses and a spectacular sight to see on its own.

The short trek to the lake allowed for new views of the cave entrances and rock arches, and once we arrived at the edge of the water, it was hard to believe we weren't on the set of a movie or in some fantasy land. To our delight, the platypuses were right where we were told they would be, frolicking in the cerulean pond. Watching them for a while was the perfect end to our visit and to the day.

We headed back to Sydney and turned in the car sometime around 8 p.m. The ride took about two hours and forty minutes with low traffic. For our entire excursion, we used less than a tank of gas and topped up just outside of the city on our way home.

Another great thing about Bayswater Car Rentals is that they have an automated return lot. So you don't have to bring the car back within working hours. As long as it's there when they come in the next morning, you're not charged for another day of rental. There's a key drop box and an automatic gate that will allow you to drop your car off in their secure lot.

The gate happened to be broken the day we were there, so they provided alternate instructions that were no more hassle to us. All in all, I found them to be extremely helpful and the process of renting a car was absolutely a breeze. Don't let transportation stop you from exploring beyond the city.

This day was a great one for us, and I'm sure you will enjoy it, too.

DAY 6 – WHALE WATCHING AND AN OVERNIGHT TRAIN TRIP

© OpenStreetMap contributors

For our final morning in Sydney, we decided to go on an adventure of another sort. This one by sea instead of by land. What we didn't realize was that it would start with an Uber ride from hell. Overall, we've always had incredible luck with our Uber drivers, so it was bound to happen eventually, right?

We'd been in Sydney for a grand total of four days, yet even I could tell you that the Circular Quay, at the heart of the entire city, is on the south side of the Harbour Bridge. Unfortunately, our Uber driver didn't seem to know that, and despite us pointing it out, she attempted to drive across the bridge heading north in rush hour traffic. The reason I mention this is because Mr. Rylon and I always build in a cushion of about three times as long as it will take to get somewhere when we have a fixed departure time. That habit—which is probably overly conservative in most situations, but who wants to rush and stress out on vacation?—saved us that morning. Well, that and our probably unwise decision to abandon our ride and jump out into the median on the highway to avoid going in that tunnel. From there, we summoned another Uber to pick us up on the side of the highway going back the correct direction.

Anyhoooooo, the reason we were so freaked out that we risked life and limb was because we had tickets on a whale watching tour that left the wharf promptly at 9:15 a.m. This entire area is a fantastic spot for visitors, filled with museums, eateries, and amazing views of the harbor and the city. It's also the primary hub for passenger vessels, including massive cruise ships. So there's a lot going on here, and our Uber couldn't get especially close to where we were supposed to meet our ship. We sprinted (okay, probably more like a fast walk for most people, but I tried my best) from where our second, much better driver left us, through the docks and onto the boat moments before they cast off the lines.

After all of that, we were in need of something relaxing like, you know…a boat ride! So we were in luck. The weather had taken a swing up. It was about 75°F. The next day spiked up to 95°F, proving why layers are your friend at that time of year. For our ride, though, it was perfect—not too hot and not too cold.

Besides, it was prime time for the humpback whale migration. The company we went with, Whale Watching Sydney (www.whalewatchingsydney.com.au), uses spotters from the air to ensure they bring you to see any animals in the area whenever possible. If you don't happen to come across any whales to watch, they will give you a ticket to come back and try again for free. Admittedly, that's not the most useful offer considering you might not be in town for long and will likely have other things planned even if you're there. Still, it shows that they're fairly confident and have a very high rate of whale sightings.

Our tour lasted for three hours and cost $54 per person. One thing I appreciated about the experience was that the animals are top priority. The tour operators won't do anything to interfere with the whales' natural behaviors or jeopardize their safety for the benefit of the guests on the boat. In fact, when we came upon a mother and calf (which was so cool!), they turned the boat off and stayed double the regulatory distance from them while we observed them.

That in no way meant we didn't get to see the whales up close, by the way. There were humpbacks all around us from the moment we reached the entrance to Sydney Harbour, just a fifteen-minute boat ride from Circle Quay. Learning how to spot them in the distance using the plumes from their blowholes, fin slapping, or large still patches on the surface was fun, especially when the captain would use people's input to steer the boat toward active groups.

When we came up to a pair of juvenile males, we again had to shut down the engines because they kept wandering closer to us of their own volition. They would dive down below the boat, where the captain could see them on his SONAR, then pop up right beside us. People would rush to the spot where they appeared to take pictures or videos from mere feet away. This went on for quite a while, until everyone had gotten a great view of the whales.

The day we went was considered extraordinarily calm by the crew on the boat. Still, someone did feed the fishes on our trip, if you know what I mean. The crew hands out seasick bags to every passenger on boarding. To me, this means that if you are prone to motion sickness, you should load up on some Dramamine at least an hour before boarding, or maybe skip this activity entirely. Between this and the winding roads, plus some adventures we haven't discussed yet, I think you'll appreciate investing in a bottle of the stuff. Nothing's worse than needing it and not having it.

After we had our fill of whale watching, we headed back to Circle Quay. Another perk of the whale watching excursion was the incredible view of the bridge, the opera house, and the city stretching out beyond them. You get treated to it twice, on the way out and while you're heading back in. The tiny specks of people all the way on the top of the Harbour Bridge emphasize just how tall the structure is (440 feet) and how brave those climbers are.

This is the perfect opportunity for an Instagram-worthy selfie.

Mr. Rylon putting up with yet another of my selfies with Sydney, the Harbour Bridge, and the Opera House in the background.

Once we were back on solid ground, we headed to the Airbnb to pack.

We probably had time to squeeze in one last activity like a tour of the SEA LIFE Aquarium (www.sydneyaquarium.com.au), a stroll through the nearby Royal Botanic Gardens (www.rbgsyd.nsw.gov.au), a visit to the Justice and Police Museum (www.sydneylivingmuseums.com.au/justice-police-museum), or a lunch at one of the many nice restaurants like Café Sydney (www.cafesydney.com) on the roof of the Customs House.

There's also a famous area called the Rocks adjacent to the Quay. Though it began as a convict settlement, this waterfront neighborhood is now known for open-air markets, cozy cobblestone lanes, funky boutiques, and the Museum of Contemporary Art (www.mca.com.au). However, knowing we'd been on the go for almost a week straight at that point, I scheduled in a break.

This is what I get.

After no more than an hour lounging around our apartment, Mr. Rylon declared he was bored. I shot him some serious side-eye, then managed to ignore him and get some work done while we waited for the next leg of our journey to start.

Roaming with the Rylons Australia and New Zealand

© OpenStreetMap contributors

This one was pretty amazing, I admit. Coming from the US, Sydney was the easiest city for us to get to, and one we wanted to visit anyway. Our primary destination was actually Melbourne, though. That's where the book signing I had come all this way to attend was being held. Instead of flying from Sydney to Melbourne, we took the overnight train, which served several purposes.

It was fun. Period.

It was less hassle. After having spent so much time on airplanes a few days before, we weren't really excited about the prospect of going through the joys of security screenings, tight timetables, the ride to the airport, uncomfortable seats, and whatever other things come with flying again. When traveling by train, you just show up and hop on the train. Easy peasy.

It saved us a night of hotel expense. I offered our host a reasonable late checkout fee to stay most of the day at our apartment. Since there wasn't anyone else checking in that day, she accepted. That gave us time to pack, take showers, and eat one last meal from our grocery haul.

Then once we were onboard the train, it was a full overnight trip, complete with single bunk beds in our sleeper compartment and a small but functional bathroom—including a shower and amenity kits—shared between us and the two-person cabin next door. I was able to sleep the entire night through, even though I was on the top bunk and a little nervous at first about falling out during the trip. It ended up reminding me of the good old days I spent on a lofted bed in my college dorm room, but more comfortable. The rocking of the train soothed me. In fact, I'd already fallen asleep before we even set the beds out and quickly went back to sleep once I was tucked in.

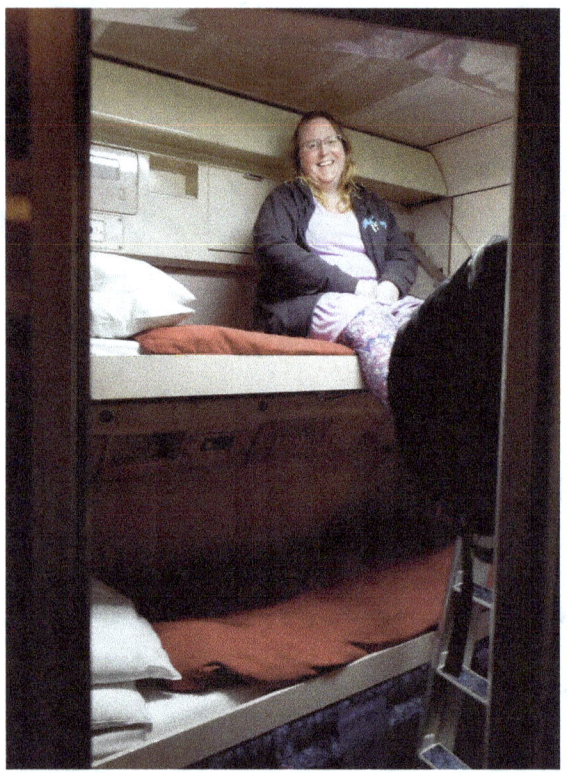

Overnight train berth with sofa made into lower bed and the upper bed folded out from the wall.

It allowed us to see more of the country. The bunk beds could be stowed so that you had a comfortable couch and plenty of overhead space, plus a big window so you could watch the world zipping by. Okay, to be honest, it was getting dark as we rolled out of the station and we only had an hour or two of daylight the next morning before we arrived in Melbourne. Even so, we were able to get a sense of the distance between the cities and a feel for the different landscapes as we made our way south. The attendant even pointed out an area where you can see mobs (yes, that's what you call a group of them!) of kangaroos hopping alongside the tracks, though we didn't happen to see any that morning.

Food was available in a separate car in the evening and an included continental boxed breakfast was delivered to us in the morning. I even tried Vegemite on the toast they provided.

If you don't already know, Vegemite is a spread made from leftover brewers' yeast. It's thick and dark like molasses, but not at all sweet. In fact, it's pungent and salty. It was okay if used *sparingly* along with some butter. At least for this first-timer.

You could buy an upgraded breakfast from the food car. Neither Mr. Rylon nor I found it necessary, as what was provided had enough variety that we could pick and choose what we liked, swap for what the other preferred, and be plenty satisfied.

If I had it to do over again, I'd book this trip in a flash. Speaking of booking…I did find out that you are not able to reserve a sleeper car ticket through NSW Trainlink's website (www.transportnsw.info/regional), although you can use that to check availability and the price, which was $181.44 per person when I bought our tickets. You will need to call them in order to make these arrangements. Their number is 4907 7501, and to dial it from the US you'd need to enter 011 (the exit code for the US) then 61 (the country code for Australia) then 2 (area code) then the phone number (the eight digits above).

Believe me, it's worth the slight inconvenience of booking by phone.

If you're booking this as soon as reservations open six months ahead of your trip, as I did and recommend you do since there's only one sleeper car per train, then sit back and enjoy your first taste of an Aussie accent. The agent who helped me was extraordinarily friendly. We both were laughing when we had to repeat ourselves multiple times. Who knew that speaking English could be so different? More on that later…

This is a phenomenal way to travel. I've taken other train trips in Europe and Asia. This was on par with those remarkable experiences. I thought it was super cool, entertaining, and peaceful all at once. There were no downsides despite a couple of my hestitancies.

A concern I had was that we weren't able to check into our next Airbnb until 2 or 3 in the afternoon. This was an issue because we had all our luggage with us, including those damn heavy suitcases bursting with books (one of the pitfalls of traveling to a book signing from across the world). However, the Southern Cross Station in Melbourne has luggage lockers available for rent.

Even better we found, was that the train company will hold your luggage in their secure and monitored storage room for the day of your journey, in either direction. They were extremely friendly and easygoing about how long and how much we could keep in there. This was a huge bonus as I didn't have to haul around even my backpack with my laptop and other valuables that I ordinarily wouldn't be comfortable leaving behind.

As you'll see in the next section, we did quite a bit of walking that morning. I'm not sure I'd have been in a very good mood if I'd had to cart all my stuff along in what turned out to be a rainy, though still enjoyable, day.

If you have the chance to travel by train in Australia (or any of the other places I've visited), you should do it. The lack of decent rail transportation in most parts of the United States is a significant shortcoming in our infrastructure as far as I'm concerned.

PART III
MELBOURNE AND THE GREAT OCEAN ROAD

DAY 7 - MELBOURNE CENTRAL

© OpenStreetMap contributors

Since we had the first half of the day to sightsee before checking into our new home away from home, I planned a walking route of the downtown highlights for our first morning in Melbourne. What I wasn't counting on was rain. Plus, I might have underestimated the distance between my points of interest.

Hey, things look a lot closer together on a map than they do when you're walking to them, especially in a chilly downpour. So here's what I'll say: if you're the kind of person who loves to powerwalk like my brother (hey, Kolin!), who works in NYC, or my mom (hey, Mom!), who speed walks for fun before the sun comes up every morning even in the snow, or my dad (hey, Dad!), who is a retired mailman, then you should definitely follow the path I'm about to set out.

However, if you aren't up for it in general or are having a lazy day, I'd skip some of the tromping around and go for the alternate course we actually took instead of the one I planned. It's good to have options and be flexible. While I always have an itinerary so that we don't waste time trying to figure out what to do, I'm almost always willing to deviate from it if conditions change or we see something we'd like to enjoy for longer than intended or figure out something isn't going to work out like I'd hoped.

So from Southern Cross, I'd planned a big rectangular path. Starting out by heading east then north, I figured we could stop by world-famous Degraves Street and Hosier Lane, which we eventually did. They ended up seeming at least three times farther than I had assumed after looking at the map, but that might have had something to do with Mr. Rylon grumbling at me continuously when he realized what I had in store for us that morning.

Sometimes happy accidents happen. He'd needed a haircut for quite some time and we stumbled across a barbershop tucked away on one of the side streets. The barber at Ossie Barber (www.facebook.com/pages/Ossies-Barber-Shop/155902417892995) was totally into his job and performed it with panache. Mr. Rylon was looking pretty spiffy and refreshed after our pit stop. Plus, the shop had a plush leather couch for me to rest on as well.

After that, we continued along our path and eventually discovered the alleyways we'd come to see. It's kind of neat that the top and most defining attraction in this city are the streets themselves. They're free, open all the time, and accessible to everyone.

What makes them so special? For one, there's an intricate warren of alleyways and lanes that hide all sorts of treasures. Art everywhere. So many cafes and bars that it would take four lifetimes to eat at every one. Nooks and crannies filled with unexpected shops, clubs, and arcades. You could easily spend an entire trip to Melbourne exploring these areas.

If, like us, you only have time to scratch the surface, what should you aim for?

Hosier Street is a feast for your eyes. Everywhere you look there is new, spectacular art to discover.

I absolutely adored Hosier Street in particular. The walls of all the buildings are blanketed in ever-changing murals. The art evolves constantly as anyone can paint over existing works with new pieces. They aren't just scribbles either—these are graffiti masterpieces. As you wander in between them, it's almost like being submerged in endless color, with something to look at in every direction.

We spent quite a while admiring the paintings and taking tons of pictures. It's crazy to think that some of that art only persists in people's snapshots as, in my opinion, some of it deserves to be on the walls of a museum. No matter how you get here, whether it's by walking from the train station in the rain or taking a short cab ride, I'd definitely say this is a must for your trip to Melbourne.

Although I have to say, finding the dang street in the warren of convoluted alleyways was half the fun, and we discovered some places along the way that we otherwise would have missed. Melbourne is truly a maze of unexpected wonders, at least in this part of the city.

So here's where we deviated from our plan. My original intention was for us to head over to the State Library of Victoria (www.slv.vic.gov.au). Not only does it look spectacular and have complimentary WiFi and well-maintained public restrooms—and you know, I am an author after all—but also, the free walking tour of Melbourne (www.imfree.com.au/melbourne) leaves from the statue of Sir Redmond Barry in front of the State Library of Victoria at 10:30 a.m. and 2:30 p.m. This tour has fantastic reviews online, as does its sister tour in Sydney. It lasts two and a half to three hours and is comprehensive. Despite their name, the tours are actually more of a "pay what you think is appropriate" kind of deal as they do collect money at the end if you are able to or feel you would like to contribute, but doing so is not mandatory to participate.

When I disclosed this portion of the day's activity to Mr. Rylon, he vetoed my plan. To be honest, I wasn't really feeling up to three hours of marching around myself, so instead we went out to lunch on Degraves Street and took a minute to regroup and devise a Plan B for the rest of the afternoon.

An interesting thing about the restaurants in this area is that they have communal seating in the center of the street, which is limited to pedestrian traffic. It's reminiscent of Parisian cafes, but the types of food served in the rows of restaurants lining the street were more varied.

In comparison to our time in Sydney, Melbourne was downright chilly, with lows in the thirties and highs in the fifties. However, umbrellas protect the tables, which are also fitted with heat lamps. So even if the weather isn't the best (as it wasn't for us) it's still a cozy place to get something eat and rest.

Fully committed to our sedentary approach to the rest of the day, we headed over to the tourist center at the corner of St. Kilda Road and Flinders Street in Federation Square (www.fedsquare.com), and found directions to one of Melbourne's trusty hop-on-hop-off buses. This time we went with City Sightseeing (www.citysightseeing.melbourne/en/times-map.htm), as their stop was less than a block away. We boarded the bus just in time, too. It poured so badly we had to abandon the partially covered upper deck of the bus and huddle inside under provided garbage-bag-quality ponchos.

I'm going to be real. I don't think we saw as much as we could have in Melbourne. Sometimes the weather, fatigue, or your health can limit you, especially on a longer trip. In this case, I didn't know it, but I was on the cusp of getting sick. I came down with some sniffles around this time that morphed into a massive respiratory infection by the time we arrived in New Zealand. I ended up dipping into my emergency stash of antibiotics by the time we settled into Auckland.

Riding the bus and tromping around in the rain that day in Melbourne probably exacerbated my situation, but I still think we got a nice overview of the city including the Royal Melbourne Zoological Gardens (www.zoo.org.au/melbourne), the giant Ferris wheel called the Melbourne Star (www.melbournestar.com), and a variety of different neighborhoods including the Italian Precinct on Lygon Street, which is credited with birthing the café culture of Melbourne. In fact, we returned there for dinner after seeing all the incredible restaurants in the area. This is also where I learned that Melbourne's sister-city is Milan, Italy. Who knew?

If I had it to do again on a sunnier day, I'd prioritize visits to Fitzroy Gardens (www.fitzroygardens.com), the Royal Botanic Gardens (www.rbg.vic.gov.au), and the Docklands, including Marvel (previously Etihad) Stadium (marvelstadium.com.au/the-stadium), as they all looked really great from the other side of the bus window.

Okay, now let's talk more about that dinner. Here's a solid recommendation: if you only have time or budget for a single nice meal in Melbourne, try your best to get reservations at Scopri (www.scopri.com.au). Including Farmhouse in Sydney, this is the second time I've had the pleasure of picking an up-and-coming restaurant that completely wowed me.

As of this writing, Tripadvisor reviews now put Scopri at the top spot over all 3,556 restaurants in the city, and I'd wholeheartedly agree with the crowd's assessment. It was phenomenal—the food, the ambiance, the service, and the price. We ate really early, as that was the only time we could get in, but also because we prefer the calm of the senior citizen hour. Our server, who was originally from Italy, gave us tons of attention and helped us assemble the meal we would enjoy the most and which also paired the best from their offerings.

Your stomach will thank you for a dinner at Scopri.

The quality of the ingredients shine here. In fact, many if not all of the vegetables and herbs are sourced from their own farm in the Maceon Ranges, which is chemical-free and run on biodynamic principles. We treated ourselves to Hervey Bay scallops in the shell with cauliflower puree and saffron herb butter; agnolotti filled with roasted rabbit, pork, and veal finished in butter and sage; potato gnocchi with spring lamb ragu; plus a cheese course, some wine for Mr. Rylon, and—of course—dessert. You will not leave this restaurant hungry, and for a while no other food will match up to your meal here.

Again, though, the quality of the food far exceeds the cost you'd expect to pay, making this as good of a value as it is a quality restaurant. For our entire two-person dinner, including food, drinks, and gratuity, we only paid $136.80 and we had leftovers to take home. A steal!

Stuffed, we returned to our Airbnb. It wasn't as charming as the place in Sydney, but it was clean and modern. It had everything you need from kitchen facilities to a washing machine, and a comfortable bed. You can check it out here. I originally selected this apartment due to its proximity to the Crown Casino Complex (www.crownmelbourne.com.au), where my book signing was being held. In comparison to the Crown Hotel, which charged a minimum of

$300 a night for a regular room with no kitchen or laundry facilities, we rented this apartment for $81 a night including cleaning charges and other fees.

The only drawback—or maybe a perk, depending on what you like—was the music blaring from the club at street level that went on until almost 4 a.m. some mornings. Mr. Rylon and I probably should have gone and partied the night away one night, but Mr. Rylon's not a dancer, I can't drink because I don't have the enzyme that processes alcohol, and—let's be honest—I had too much stuff on my itinerary for the next day to be up all night!

DAY 8 - THE GREAT OCEAN ROAD

© OpenStreetMap contributors

This was one of my favorite days of our entire trip. Now, that's like saying I like lemon raspberry cheesecake more than birthday cake ice cream, because really...it's all great. But still, this day was remarkable even by the high standards of the rest of the fun-filled adventures we had in Australia and New Zealand.

So of course, I'm telling you that no visit to Melbourne is complete without an outing along the Great Ocean Road. However, there are a lot of options on how you can tour it. For ultimate flexibility, you could rent a car and do it yourself, stopping wherever you like for as long as you like. You could take a large tour bus, which is probably the most affordable option.

However, what I recommend is opting for a van tour. There are several operators who take small groups of 8-10 people and offer a personalized experience. This is what we did. Our driver/guide, who told us to call him Rob-O, arranged to pick us up at our Airbnb at the crack of dawn. He made the day so easy for us. We didn't have to worry about navigating or hours of driving—be prepared, this is a *long* day and a lot of car time. Plus, there's no way we would have learned as much as we did from our guide if we'd simply followed the same route on our own.

We booked our tour through Escape Discovery Tours (www.escapediscoveryadventures.com.au) for $116.22 per person. Our tickets included tea and snacks in the morning, a full lunch at a restaurant along the way, and a bag of local snacks—which alternately makes for fun souvenirs to give people back home—for the return trip. In addition, our driver narrated as he took us from place to place over the course of fourteen hours. Yes, the tour lasted from 7 a.m. to 9 p.m.! Considering what you would have paid for a rental car, the added local knowledge, and the included meals, I feel like it was money well spent. However, if you'd rather be independent, I'll tell you about the places we saw that I thought were the best so you can stop off there if you like.

Once we were onboard the van, which was roomy and comfortable, there were about six other people along for the ride. We got to know them throughout the day, so that added another layer to the tour that we wouldn't have experienced if we'd ventured out on our own.

As we headed out of the city past canary-yellow fields bursting with blossoming canola (rapeseed) plants, Rob-O told us what to expect for the day. I liked that although we drove over three hundred miles in total, we stopped every hour or so at various points of interest, which actually made it seem like we weren't on such a long drive. Besides, our guide was hilarious and told us stories while we were in motion so we learned a lot and were definitely entertained along the way.

We wandered around the beach at Urquhart Bluff before getting educated on the Tim Tam slam.

Our first stop was at Urquhart Bluff. It's a wide, sandy, crescent beach south of Anglesea. As we wandered around and enjoyed the sound of the waves rolling in, Rob-O prepared a breakfast tea and a spread of snacks for everyone. While we gathered around the picnic table and warmed our hands, we learned about the military men who built the Great Ocean Road after they returned from World War I. The country employed the men, who constructed this 151 mile long Australian National Heritage monument. It is the longest war memorial in the world.

This works project served two purposes. It created a way for people to travel the far southeastern coast. More importantly, it enabled its builders to form a support system of other soldiers to help them acclimate to life after the war and cope with what we'd today identify as PTSD. Maybe this is a romanticized view of what really happened, but I could see where this would be a beautiful place to recover after the horrors of war, especially since the Australian and New Zealand Army Corps (ANZAC) troops didn't fare very well in battle. They had never fought in a major international conflict before they faced down the Ottoman Empire in the Battle of Gallipoli with heavy losses. The anniversary of this battle, April 25th, is recognized in Australia as ANZAC Day in remembrance of military lives lost.

I'm not sure why, maybe because I've always been an avid reader and now make up stories for a living, but these sorts of accounts in history books never really sink in to my brain. Travel is one way that I develop an understanding of, and have context for, these important events I probably learned about in school even if I no longer remember studying them (sorry, teachers). I felt the same way when I stood on the D-Day beaches in France and in an ancient temple in China. But those are tales for another guidebook...

Lest you think the entire day was either sad or aimed only at warfare buffs, we learned another, much sillier life skill on this stop—how to perform a Tim Tam slam. This is critical to your time in Australia and should be a priority for anyone visiting Down Under. First, the cookies. Tim Tams are an Australian staple. They're a long, rectangular, wafer-y biscuit with various flavored fillings that are then dunked in chocolate. I'm really not doing them justice here. They're right up there with Girl Scout Cookies on the crack-snack scale. My favorite is the chewy caramel kind. By writing this I've made myself crave them and the cartons we brought home in our suitcases after we emptied out all the books are long gone. Almost worth making another trip to Australia just for these!

Anyway, if you bite off one corner of a Tim Tam and then the corner diagonal from it, you create a temporary straw. People who like coffee (sorry, I'm a tea drinker) will then stick one end of the Tim Tam in their mug, slurp a bit through the cookie, then shove the whole thing in their mouth quickly as it starts to melt and dissolve. Apparently it's pretty close to heaven, so give it a try and be sure to allocate some luggage space for a stash big enough that you have some for yourself as well as gifts for others. They make an awesome souvenir.

The beach made a lovely classroom for all of this education, though after a few cups of tea I realized I might be in for an uncomfortable ride. Not to fear! There were public bathroom facilities here, though as Rob-O told us, they were at best two-star rated. I had some terrifying visions of going into this rustic bathroom and becoming the victim of all those deadly snakes and spiders you hear about living in Australia. I'm happy to report in our entire trip, not only on the Great Ocean Road, we didn't see a single dangerous creature outside of the zoo. So don't let that possibility damper your enthusiasm for exploration or lead to you peeing your pants because you're afraid of what might be lurking in the bathroom stall!

At this point we were able to wander around the area for a bit before piling back in the van and heading for our next stop, which was a picture opportunity with the archway and statues at the beginning of the official Great Ocean Road.

As an avid photographer, I really appreciated that we stopped at the most scenic and iconic places along our route. We were able to take tons of pictures and stretch our legs from time to time. I think the tour was extremely well balanced and made the experience very enjoyable. Another example of this was a brief stop to enjoy the view in Lorne, a picturesque resort town.

The view overlooking Lorne is spectacular.

The ocean was ever present during the day, just off the left of our van. That view never got old. Though the cliff, the spectacular landscape, and the curve-hugging Great Ocean Road were themselves the main attractions, we did add more and more perks along the way. We discovered the next at Kennett River, a tiny seaside town with a population of just 41 people. Here we were educated about koalas in their natural environment and how to spot them in the tall eucalyptus trees.

Okay, so mostly they look like a beehive or a gray rock wedged in the crotch of a tree. They climb pretty high and generally are tucked in a ball sleeping. Not super exciting on the surface. I hope you were able to visit the Featherdale Wildlife Park to get a good up-close look at the animals and maybe even pet one yourself. Though this experience was entirely different, we did observe real live wild koalas, damn it! In fact, from that point on, it became a game to spot them from the bus as we drove through more wooded areas.

Again, I was impressed by the sheer volume and variety of birds in Australia. This stop really hammered that home. It was one of the things that made this country seem so different to us. The bird sounds—chirps, whistles, and cooing—were completely different from what we're used to, and the vibrant colors on many of the species there are stunning.

Like Featherdale back in Sydney but on a whole new level, the birds in Kennett River are free to come and go as they please. They're wild animals, not captive ones. However, they have been bribed repeatedly by tourists and tour operators to become far more familiar with humans than they would be naturally.

For the record, I don't support the feeding of wild animals, which alters their natural behaviors, doesn't provide the diet they require, and makes them more susceptible to predators. However, even without a fistful of birdseed, you couldn't help but be swarmed by gorgeous king parrots, cockatoos, crimson rosellas, and kookaburras as you were koala hunting here. These are birds we'd likely only see in pet stores or zoos back home. Be prepared for a close encounter or ten with these magnificent birds if you opt to peek in at Kennett River.

Mr. Rylon made some new friends in Kennett River.

In fact, they will land right on you, including on your head.

For this reason, I would highly recommend a hat. Although I didn't see anyone get hit with a bird-crap bomb, I'm positive it happens often. I wouldn't let that keep me from experiencing this place, which was truly incredible, but I would take a few precautions. No one wants to be riding around covered in poop for the eleven or so hours you have left before you finish the circuit and head back to Melbourne.

Rob-O had a decent amount of time to talk during our next leg as we wound our way toward Apollo Bay. Through his headset mic at the front of the van I have to say, the guy cracked me up. He certainly kept us from getting bored. One of his valuable bits of information as we drove past awe-inspiring seaside view after view was on translating Aussie-talk. So here's my take. Just because you speak English does not mean you're going to understand a damn thing that Australian people are saying to you.

They have a way of communicating that made me feel like the uncool kid who didn't know a single word of slang. Like maybe I came from the 1800's or something. Many of their words seem to be sing-songish nicknames. Here are some helpful rules to help you through your adventure—credit to Rob-O, of course, whose very name proves my point.

Step #1 – Abbreviate everything.

Step #2 – Put a vowel sound on the end of everything.

Here are some examples...

- Robert = Rob-O
- Garbage man = garbo
- Afternoon = arvo
- Breakfast = brekkie
- Chocolate = choccy
- McDonalds = maccas
- ACDC = acadaca
- Laptop = lappy
- Devastated = devo
- Mosquito = mozzie
- Sunglasses = sunnies
- Expensive = exxy
- Conversation = convo

Whew! I think you get the point. All kidding aside, it does take a while to decipher what people are saying sometimes, especially when they string a bunch of these Australianisms together really quickly.

So back to our van trip...

We stopped for lunch at a cute café in Apollo Bay—a town much bigger than Kennett River, though quieter and quainter than nearby Lorne—called Waves. The portions were downright American-sized, so when Rob-O told us each person got to pick something off the menu, Mr. Rylon went for a savory panini and I—duh—picked a dessert crepe filled with fruit and sweet goo. Then we divvied everything up and shared it. It was plenty for us both.

The bakery here has some pretty spectacular treats that weren't included in our lunch, so make sure you check out the pastry case while you're waiting on your food if you're on the tour. The schedule is pretty tight to hit all these stops, so after lunch you might not have time to stand in line and get a treat for the road if you don't do it when you first go inside.

In addition, thanks to a recommendation from Rob-O, I tried my first extra spicy Bundaberg ginger beer. If that's your kind of thing, you should really try it. It's not overly sugary, but really flavorful and packs a punch. Non-alcoholic drinks by this manufacturer are produced in Queensland and widely available across Australia. After that day I picked it up every chance I got.

After lunch we kept going along the winding road. Though the views were always of the ocean, it never got old. Sometimes we were high on cliffs and sometimes down at the water's edge. There were also dips inland over small bridges that spanned winding creeks. Everywhere you looked, it was scenic. At this point we realized we were as far south as we'd ever been in our lives, next stop Tasmania and then Antarctica. It felt like it too. In September, it was pretty darn chilly and windy and got more so as we went on with the day. The high was only 50°F.

The climate here changes quite a bit, too. There's one small section of the road that veers away from the sea. Don't be discouraged when trees replace the water outside your window. First, because you can spot more koalas. But mostly because this is an exceptionally rare type of ecosystem—a temperate rainforest. Translation: it's super green and jungley, but not hot and steamy. When I think back to my mental picture of Australia as a charred, hot, orange island, devoid of vegetation, I realize how wrong I was. Sure, the outback might be polar opposite of where we were then, but most of the places we visited were verdant and lush.

Tucked into the Great Otway National Park, there's a half-mile wooden boardwalk at Mait's Rest (https://parkweb.vic.gov.au/explore/parks/great-otway-national-park/things-to-do/maits-rest) that allows you to take a leisurely walk through this incredible biome. Both Mr. Rylon and I thought this was a sneak attack sort of place. You don't expect it to be magical, but it was exactly that.

Mait's Rest was an unexpected bonus to our Great Ocean Road day trip.

Honestly, this was such a cool experience. The trees here were enormous! They're a mix of towering myrtle beech (one nearly four-hundred years old!), enormous eucalyptus, and lush fern trees. They are impressive! From the ground, the tops of the trees were lost in the clouds. Judging by how huge they were at the base, they seemed to stretch up for miles.

The ferns and other plants were also unbelievable. I felt like I might see a stegosaurus stomp past any moment. Combined with short bridges over streams and fascinating birds (where are there not birds in Australia?), this was a must-see stop.

Rob-O conveyed lots of information about the rainforest, too. In fact, there was a killer among us!

A flesh-eating animal.

Don't worry too much. You're not likely to see one of these endangered Otway black snails, never mind get consumed by one. You should be aware, though, if you tackle this walk after lunch, that there is no restroom at Mait's Rest. You're going to have to wait until you get to the crowning jewel of the day at the next stop.

After that we...yep, climbed back in the van. I know it sounds like a lot of driving around, and honestly it was a concern for me when I booked this excursion, but it was broken up and never got tedious. There's so much to see and the company was good, too. By now we were on friendly terms with the other couples and guests on the tour and spent the time in between destinations in easy conversation.

Finally, *finally*, we arrived at the site I'd thought the whole journey was about: the Apostles (https://parkweb.vic.gov.au/explore/parks/twelve-apostles-marine-national-park)! No, not like Mark, Matthew, and the rest of that gang. These Apostles are limestone pillars standing out in the Southern Ocean. Enormous limestone pillars. There aren't twelve of them—there are eight since the ninth collapsed in 2005—so don't bother trying to figure out why they're called this. Truth is, they used to be named the Sow and Piglets until Aussie tourism boards figured the Apostles sounded better. So there you have it.

Many companies, including our tour operator, offered a helicopter ride at this stop. While I believe it would be a spectacular vantage point, the view from the ground is pretty great. Plus the wind was absolutely shrieking off the coast the day we were there.

Don't believe me? Check out this video of Mr. Rylon and me (https://www.facebook.com/jayne.rylon/videos/1690446930966488) and you'll get a sense of what it was like to face the full force of the gales on that day.

It's not a place I'd really feel comfortable hopping into a helicopter, unless it was calm and perfect weather for this area, which of course you can never predict. It seems like a really expensive option to risk in this location, so I'd recommend skipping that and seeing the Apostles from the lookout point which was breathtaking (and not only because of the stabbing wind!).

Sometimes imperfect weather can make for dramatic pictures like they did this day at The Apostles.

From the parking lot, it's about a ten-minute walk—at Jayne-and-Mr.-Rylon pace, and including a detour to the restrooms—to get to the viewing platform. Be sure to have your selfie game on point because you're not going to find many backgrounds more dramatic than this one. I actually loved that the sky and ocean were fierce on the day we were there because it stirred up the water and made the waves very dramatic.

There's an adjacent site called Loch Ard Gorge (https://parkweb.vic.gov.au/explore/parks/port-campbell-national-park/things-to-do/loch-ard-gorge) where you can walk down several steep and narrow staircases along the sheer vertical walls of the gorge to the water's edge. I've heard that in the summer you could swim or even SCUBA dive here, but trusty Rob-O told us he wouldn't risk it most days. It was a laughable idea on the day we were there, with monstrous waves that made it easy to imagine the shipwreck that occurred here back in June of 1878, giving the gorge its name.

Tom Pearce and Eva Carmichael, both teenagers, were the only survivors. Tom washed up on shore, then heard Eva's cries and raced back into the ocean to save her. Unfortunately, there was no way out of the gorge, so Tom climbed up and flagged down help.

In my romance author brain, I'd created a whole *Titanic*-worthy love affair for these two, but it's told that even though both survived, they never spoke again after they were rescued. Eva returned to England and married a wealthy man, while Tom was a sailor for the rest of his life, until he died thirty years later.

Ah well, that's why I get to make stuff up for my other job. It guarantees a happy ending for everyone!

These days, the gorge is beautiful to behold. The cliffs make two arms that protrude out from the beach, angled toward each other so that there's only a small gap in between them. When down on the soft, wide beach, you feel as if you're in a rock bowl. There's even a shallow cave you can peek into for a glimpse of the limestone formations dangling from the ceiling. On a nicer day —it had started to rain in addition to the whipping wind—this would be a great spot for a picnic.

From here, things speed up. Don't worry, you'll be pretty pooped by this point in the day. Instead of winding along the coast for long return journey, the tour cut inland and took a direct route on the highway back to Melbourne. Fortunately, they also provided us each with a bag brimming with Australian snacks. I hoarded some of mine and used them as souvenirs for people back home.

Rob-O was quieter on the way back, which I think most people appreciated. I might have been the only person awake at one point. I took the opportunity to check emails, upload photos from the day to social media, and pretend like I wasn't coming down with a chest cold.

We did make a brief stop to hit up some bathrooms on the final sprint to Melbourne, but it didn't seem like very long at all until we were rolling up to our Airbnb again and saying goodbye to the awesome people we'd met that day.

Here's where I'd normally tell you about a restaurant that I recommend. This tour was amazing but also long and tiring. When we finished it, neither Mr. Rylon nor I felt like going out or preparing our own food.

So here's my next tip! If you're having one of these days, Melbourne has several delivery options that will bring you food from one of their many fabulous restaurants. Of course there's Ubereats, but also one called Deliveroo, which we found had the greatest variety of options close to where we were staying.

So just because you feel like hanging out on the couch in your pajamas doesn't mean you can't sample some of the cuisine the city is well known for before crashing hard.

DAY 9 - QUEEN VICTORIA MARKET

Despite our action-packed previous day, we kicked this morning off early. I had to check in and set up my table at the book signing we'd traveled all this way to attend in the afternoon, so we wanted to squeeze in some sightseeing before business. However, I'd recommend that you hit this destination early as well since some of the best finds might be gone as the day progresses.

Yes, I'm talking about the Queen Victoria Market (https://qvm.com.au). This place is enormous and chock full of food, souvenirs, clothing, toys, and even live chickens. I don't suggest you try to smuggle one of those home, though!

If I had it to do over again, I'd have made sure to visit the market on my first day in town so we could have stocked up our kitchen with fresh ingredients. There were stalls overflowing with fresh and healthy produce, eggs—from a variety of birds like chickens and ducks and more—candy, premade trail mixes, and even prepared meals. Everything was very reasonably priced.

I regret that we didn't try some of the more unusual egg offerings, but we didn't think they would survive in our backpack.

So when you go, bring a backpack and a cold bag to store things in, and you'll be set to cook great meals and save some money on dining out at the same time.

Be prepared for a lot of walking on the concrete floor. Wear your comfy shoes for this one. If you go up and down each of the twenty or so aisles, you could easily walk around here for two to three hours as we did.

One perk, since we underestimated how much we would find to buy here and many of the vendors don't accept credit cards, is that there is an ATM at the center of the market space. The withdrawal fees were a better bargain than the crappy exchange rates listed at any of the official exchange offices we passed while in the city, too.

There's also a food court here that features street vendors, small restaurants housed in storage containers, and food trucks if you get hungry while you're shopping.

From here we had to head back to Southbank and lug a bazillion pounds of books through the winding corridors of the Crown Entertainment Complex (www.crownmelbourne.com.au), which features a gigantic casino, a wide range of restaurants, a spa, movie theaters, an arcade, and live performances, in addition to events like the book signing I attended. If you enjoy gambling, you will love meandering through the complex and trying your luck at the games. Mr. Rylon wandered off from our event space under the guise of changing some American money into Australian dollars at the cage's cashier so that I could make change for people buying books, and mysteriously disappeared for an hour or so. In his defense, he came back with more money than he left with, so I suppose that's okay.

He said the casino itself was largely the same as ones he's experienced in the US at places like Las Vegas. The only notable difference was the abundance of games with themes tailored to Asian customers. So for American or European visitors, some of the graphics or concepts might be novel compared to those you've seen before.

Mr. Rylon also discovered that the casino cashier offers a decent exchange rate since they want you to take out more money to play there. Add that to the list of places I would exchange money before ever using an official currency exchange shop, especially one at an airport.

The area the casino is located in on Southbank also offers a ton of things to see and do around the Crown complex. Wandering up and down the river here, you'll see street performers, hear live music, and pass more restaurants than you could hope to try in ten visits.

The atmosphere of this neighborhood makes it vibrant. It's a great place to pass an afternoon.

DAY 10 - FICTIONALLY YOURS, MELBOURNE, LUNA PARK, AND ST. KILDA

This day of my itinerary was entirely filled with meeting friendly, enthusiastic readers at Fictionally Yours, Melbourne (www.fictionallyyoursmelbourne.com). While this might not apply to many of you reading this, I want to give a shout out to the event organizers Tina Gephart and Penny Rudge, who graciously invited me Down Under for one of the best experiences of my writing career. They put on this event every other year. Having attended many book signings and conferences, I can honestly say this is the cream of the crop.

If you enjoy reading, definitely check it out. Be sure to do so well in advance, as tickets are limited. They sell out over a year ahead of the event. However, the organizers are amazing and help people who can't attend sell their tickets to others who would like to go, so join their Facebook group here for more info on that.

If you're reading this because you're considering arranging a trip around the FYM book signing, hello! DO IT! I can't stress that enough. For international readers and those of you who live in Australia alike, this is an experience you won't regret. At the signing itself you can meet your favorite romance authors, get your books (or a scrapbook or anything else you like) autographed, load up on swag, and discover plenty of new things to read.

There are so many fantastic authors who join in the festivities that there are two separate days of book signings, with half of the authors featured on each day. Then after the final signing, the organizers throw an after party. Sure, they had an open bar. But I just have two words for you about this shindig:

donut wall. Yes, there was an entire *wall* of donuts. And while the specifics might vary by year, the event is sure to be incredible with two of the most dedicated and super-cool hosts you could ask for.

For the rest of you, who aren't interested in romance novel book signings (though you should give it a try, you just might like it!), I had quite a few other activities on my short list that I would have pursued if I hadn't been busy this day.

If you don't mind getting up early (you need to arrive before 6 a.m.), or heights, the hot air balloon rides (www.globalballooning.com.au/melbourne/flight/melbourne-balloon-flight) offered over the city or the Yarra Valley wine region sounded like a once-in-a-lifetime experience. Hold on to your wallets. They will be significantly lighter during your flight, because this was one of the priciest activities I researched. A one-hour ride will set you back about $500 per person. Also, the schedule is extremely dependent on the weather, for good reason, of course. No one's vacation would be enhanced by plunging to your death due to a storm popping up!

Be aware that most of the operators do not refund your money in the case of inclement weather and instead will allow you to reschedule your tour. Therefore, if you pursue this option... First, send me a picture and let me know how it was, because I'm jealous! Second, schedule it at the front end of your time in Melbourne so that if there is a cancellation, you can shuffle things around and reschedule before moving on and losing out on your fees.

If all that is too much for you, another option would be to explore the St. Kilda (stkildamelbourne.com.au) area including Luna Park (lunapark.com.au), penguin watching (stkildapenguins.com.au), and more spectacular beachfront.

No matter what you choose to spend your time on, be sure to regroup for one last meal at an independent restaurant before you leave this foodie-friendly city. At least that's what we did, because we knew that once we left Australia, the style of travel we had planned for New Zealand would be entirely different.

But more about that in a few "days."

DAY 11 - RIVERBOAT CRUISES AND FLY TO AUCKLAND

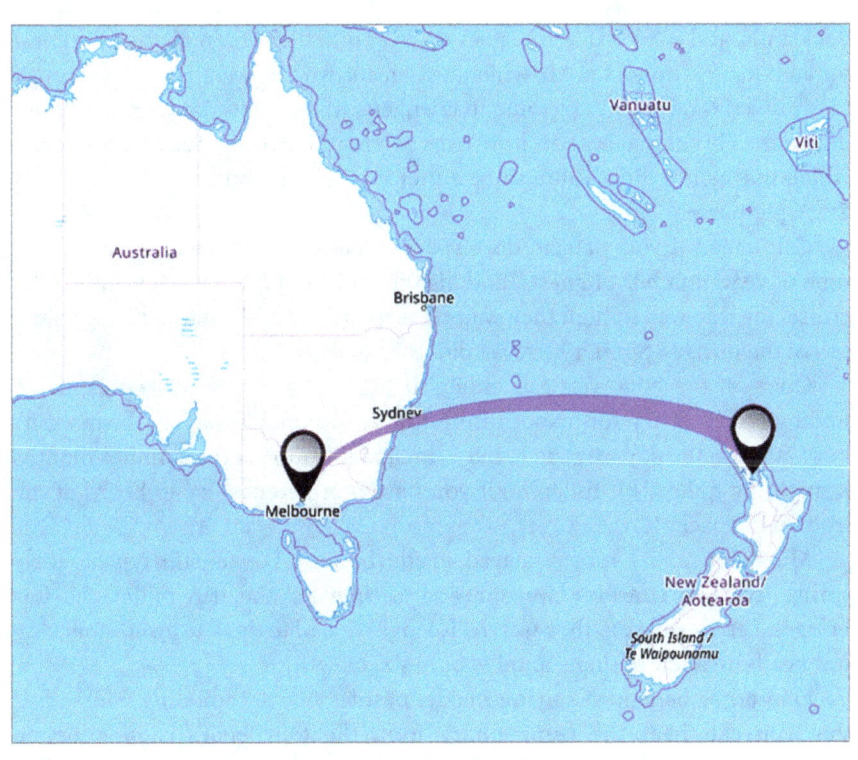

© OpenStreetMap contributors

It was already *that* day. Our final day in Australia! The time had flown by. So after repacking our significantly lighter luggage (thank goodness Tim Tams weigh less than books!) and tidying up around the apartment, we picked a few last things we wanted to do before we headed off.

One of them was a riverboat cruise on the Yarra River, which bisects Melbourne. The Melbourne City Cruises (www.melbcruises.com.au) starting point was near our apartment in Southbank. We probably should have walked there, but we weren't sure exactly where it was, so we let the Uber driver figure that out. Just so you know, it's located at Berth 5 of the Southbank Promenade between the Evan Walker and Princes bridges.

Everything about this cruise was very laidback and relaxing. They have quite a few sail times every day and several different route options. Although I had a specific one in mind (of course I did), a more relaxed traveler could stroll up any day and time and probably have a decent option not too far in the future.

There is an "A" cruise, which goes down the river toward the ports and docklands, and a "B" cruise that goes up river into the garden district. Both last for an hour. We opted for AB, which just means we first went one way, stopped to drop off and pick up some passengers, then continued in the other direction. This cruise lasted a little over two hours and cost $24.87 per person, which makes it a great value since either of the one-hour cruises alone cost $17.76 per person.

Call ahead if you want to do a specific tour, as the schedule changes by time of year, number of guests, and also the tide. On the day we went for the cruise, the tide was so high they weren't sure they'd be able to make it under a few of the bridges. Spoiler alert: we did.

Once on the boat, you can either sit inside the glass-enclosed cabin on folding chairs or try for a spot in the limited outdoor area. The boat wasn't busy at all on the day we rode it, but I can imagine during the summer months it might be quite a bit fuller. So if you have a preference, try to board at the front of the pack.

Mr. Rylon and I mostly stayed inside because it was still typical early spring weather. However, we did ride outside for the trip under the low bridges. Let me tell you, they weren't joking! We had to duck to avoid smacking our heads on a few of them, and I'm only 5'2" tall.

One other benefit to staying inside, besides not decapitating yourself, is that you can hear the commentary from the tour boat's captain better. While I enjoy walking around and exploring a city on my own, I do feel like getting information straight from locals, especially those who do this for a living, always paints a richer picture than what you could observe on your own.

Just as the hop-on-hop-off bus is a go-to for getting an overview of cities, I feel like river cruises are always a fantastic way to see the heart of a city from a different perspective. The waterways are often right at the center of the action and most of the important buildings will be visible, with unobstructed views from the water.

Melbourne is no different.

Melbourne on a sunny spring day is great to explore by boat.

After we'd wrapped up here, we hustled back to our apartment, collected our bags, and headed off to the airport. We were a bit early, but again...you never know if a mob of kangaroos might storm the city and prevent us from leaving or something like that. Besides, we had a special indulgence for ourselves lined up and wanted to take full advantage of it.

You see, when I was booking this part of the trip, I realized that there was a particular flight, late at night, where pricing on business class seats was pretty damn reasonable. At least compared to the trans-Pacific ones that were the cost of a car, remember? So I hopped right on that and plunked down $635 for lay-flat business seats. Our flight was from 6 p.m. to midnight, so we got a gourmet dinner including ice cream, time to relax, and a comfy spot to fully recline while doing it.

That's a clear example of where, yes, we spent more than we had to, but it was a nice balance between splurge and value compared to the $245.71 each we would have spent on economy seats anyway. That would have landed us on a plane where there are three seats minimum in each section. Again, one of us would have been squished in the middle the whole way to New Zealand.

Besides, Mr. Rylon is *obsessed* with flying first class. So a chance to try out business class on one of these international flights (even if it was a short-haul international flight) was a big deal to him. Not going to lie, I enjoyed it, too. Especially because I was starting to get sicker and the pressure in my head and chest was discomfort enough to deal with right then.

Another consideration that went into making this decision was that we would have had to pay excess baggage fees in economy due to the suitcases we brought for the book signing. So add that to the dinner we got onboard, which included some decent Australian and New Zealand wines for Mr. Rylon and…

Well, it wasn't such a bad deal.

Let's rewind for a second. Drinks. Food. Value.

These are all things you can leverage to get the most out of your money if you do treat yourself to one of these upper class flights. Arrive at the airport early enough to use the airline's business class lounge. The food provided for free in some of them, like Air New Zealand's, is better than you might think. There's a wide variety of offerings. Plus, for those of you who drink, alcohol is complimentary.

While I'm not suggesting you get hammered before your flight—please don't—consuming a beverage or two that you would have purchased at airport prices definitely helps reduce the gap in the costs some more.

So let's talk about those lay-flat seats for a minute. Was it worth it?

On this flight…absolutely. For the price of a small car…still nope.

Let's face it, there isn't *that* much more room than we had in the Skycouch section. To be fair, our meal and flight time didn't allow for us to turn the seat into a bed and actually sleep (which may have been why they were relatively inexpensive), so maybe I'd feel differently on a longer flight. Then again, I'd never be able to justify the cost of a lay-flat seat on a trip of a greater duration, so…yeah, the benefit is limited.

Mr. Rylon better not get used to business class!

Plus, the way these seats are constructed, each one is nestled into its own pod. That means if you're traveling with someone, you're isolated from them. That wasn't so bad for me. For some people, like Mr. Rylon (if you recall, he's afraid of flying), that could be an issue. Usually we hold hands during takeoff and landing (aww) to help him stay calm. If you think I'm reaching here to make myself feel better about flying in economy or premium economy most of the time, you're probably right. After all, he did just fine kicked back in his comfy pod.

Still, nothing is perfect.

On arrival in New Zealand, I completed the obligatory cell phone SIM card swaperoo despite the late hour and my incessant coughing. Then we were out of there. The airport in Auckland isn't very big, which makes it convenient both for departures and arrivals. Transiting through it (as we did on the way to Australia) is also a breeze.

The airport has a shuttle that will take you to any of the nearby hotels. It is called the Skybus (www.skybus.co.nz) and cost us $4.50 per person. Service to the international terminal runs 24 hours a day. The bus comes every half hour, and you can buy tickets online or at automated kiosks at the bus stop. This sounds super convenient, and truly, most times it is. Except at midnight, with a serious respiratory infection, standing outside in the cold after barely having missed the bus was something I'm getting too old for (I'm 38, but you get my point).

I'm not ashamed to admit I hailed a taxi. The driver didn't seem to want my fare and encouraged me to take the bus. When pressed, they said they'd charge us $20 to drive us the mile or two to the hotel. I sort of wished I'd done it anyway. Refer back to the cost benefit discussion from earlier. I *really* wanted to be asleep right then.

However, for the vast majority of times and circumstances, the shuttle is great. We gladly took it on our return journey at the end of our trip. We had something special planned for the next week of adventuring, but for the few hours we would need to sleep before starting out on that leg of the trip, I had booked a room at the nearby Ibis Budget Airport Hotel (www.accorhotels.com/gb/hotel-7865-ibis-budget-auckland-airport/index.shtml) for $73.46.

Once the bus arrived, we were there within minutes. The hotel was simple and clean, practical and cost effective. They had us checked in and on our way efficiently. It had everything we needed, if not a lot of space to walk around. That didn't matter, since all I did was take three steps inside and crash face-down on the bed until the sun stabbed through the window at dawn.

Time for the next phase of Vacation Boot Camp!

PART IV

AUCKLAND AND THE NORTH ISLAND OF NEW ZEALAND

DAY 12 - AUCKLAND TO WAITOMO

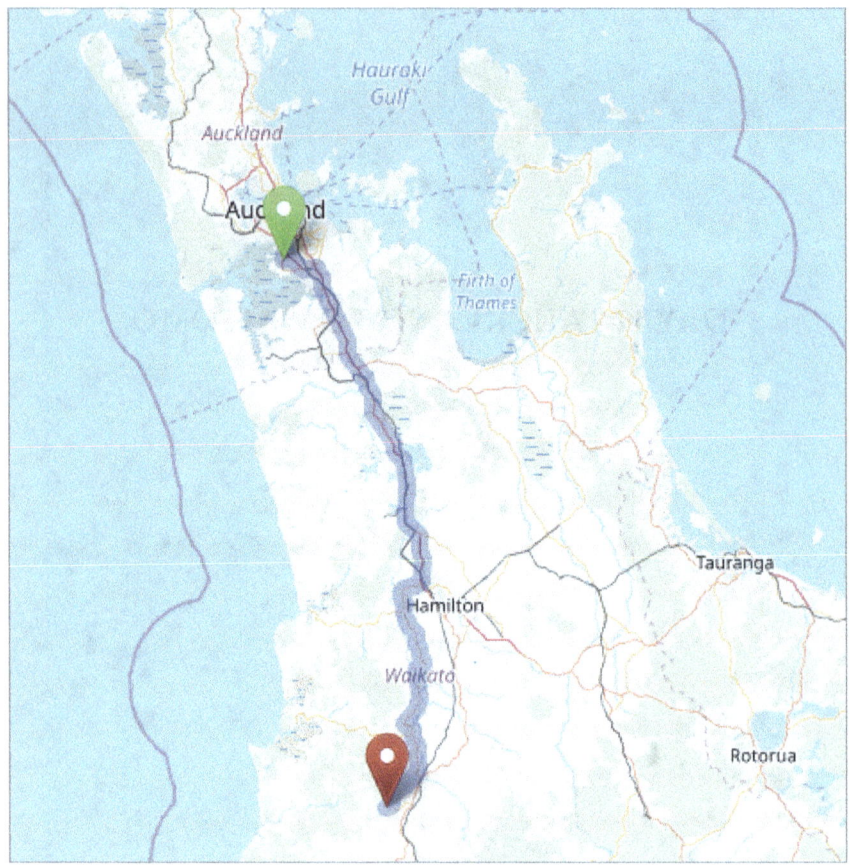

© OpenStreetMap contributors

I woke up eager to explore a whole new country, right after I coughed up a lung. Fortunately, the Ibis provides a hot beverage station in each room so I could swallow a handful of antibiotics from my emergency stash. If you are planning to travel abroad, especially to areas more remote than Australia and New Zealand (Mr. Rylon and I sometimes find ourselves on islands like Aitutaki in the South Pacific while SCUBA diving), then I suggest you talk to your doctor about setting up your own travel medicine kit with a few essentials. In this case, I guarantee it saved me a trip to a clinic and salvaged our vacation. Although it took me three or four more days to get back to normal(ish), I was still able to go sightseeing and enjoy the week.

So...New Zealand. It's a country comprised of two main islands, conveniently referred to as the North and South Islands, located about 900 miles east of Australia. It has shocking variety in its landscapes, which range from geothermal wonderlands, to mountains and fiords, redwood forests, rolling pastures, and gorgeous coastal regions. Its rich culture is anchored by the traditions of the Māori people, who settled the islands around 1300AD. This makes the names of places here super fun to try to pronounce. Everywhere you look, you'll see something more beautiful than the previous incredible spot that enticed you to haul out your camera and take picture after picture.

To me, the ambiance felt modern and advanced, but with a lingering attitude of independence and a definite slant toward to-each-their-own that was, frankly, refreshing. Of all the places I've been in the world, this is one I could easily imagine myself calling home or at least returning to visit over and over. It had plenty of conveniences and yet was very laidback.

For example, we were there during their elections. What a difference compared to the US during political season. The largest debate in the newspaper was about who had the best shoes, with a pair of snakeskin winklepickers in the lead. The prime minister who won, Jacinda Ardern, is the youngest female head of government—elected at 37 years old—and was the first world leader to give birth while in office. Overall, the country reflected this progressive mindset.

In addition to few clean, interesting cities there are lots of rural areas to explore. It's an ideal vacation destination.

Before I tell you all about our adventures in New Zealand, I first want to give you some context for one of the major decisions we made—to rent a campervan and live in it for the week we spent here. Kiwis seem to be obsessed with van life. I admit, the idea of jamming ourselves into a tiny house on wheels and bopping around the country didn't sound that appealing until I did a ton of research and realized that New Zealand is perfectly set up with everything you need to make this style of travel work. They have all the facilities you'll need to be comfortable and, in fact, you'll get to see more of the country than you would if you needed to divert off the trail to find a place to stay instead of bringing your own temporary home with you. It's sort of like going to Ireland and staying in a series of bed and breakfasts. It's the generally accepted thing to do, a way of experiencing this place that makes your trip complete. You should definitely do it.

Unlike in the United States—where RVing brings to mind a bazillion hours on the road in between awesome sights—New Zealand is a very manageable size for touring. After we arrived at our first destination, we never spent more than two hours or so in the campervan getting to our next destination. This excludes the ride from Auckland to our initial stop and from our final point back to Auckland, but even that was only about a three-hour trip each way.

I'm getting ahead of myself.

Renting, driving, and staying in a campervan in New Zealand is not only a painless process, it is also the only way you can immerse yourself in some of the more remote areas. This is especially true of the South Island. Unfortunately, Mr. Rylon and I decided early on that with only a week to explore—and given the fact that it was barely spring and, therefore, exceptionally cold and snowy on the South Island—that we were going to stick to the North Island on this trip. As it turned out, we only covered about half of that because another advantage you have when traveling this way is ultimate freedom. You can do as much or as little as you want in a day without having to worry about rushing to reach whatever accommodations you've booked for that night.

We loved New Zealand enough that we would absolutely go back. Someday, we hope to do even more sightseeing on the North Island in addition to discovering the entire South Island as well. Given our time constraint and being first-timers to the country, I'm thrilled with what we managed to jam into our week. I would recommend this itinerary to other people who want a taste of a bunch of different facets of the country. Just think of this as your New Zealand sampler pack so that next time you visit you can take a deeper dive into the things you enjoy most.

If you're a skier or like to hike or have particular interests that correlate with a specific region of New Zealand, then you might be better off picking a spot to stay put in. Otherwise, I say go for the campervan and cover as much ground as you can during your visit in true Vacation Boot Camp style.

Another bonus, campervans are very affordable to rent and insure. This is in part due to an even better exchange rate against the US dollar than the Australian dollar has. At the time I'm writing this, one American dollar is worth 1.48 New Zealand dollars, so your buck has nearly one and a half times as much bang there. Our total cost for the week was $837.31, which works out to $119.62 per day for both lodging and transportation. Not bad at all, especially considering you will also save on meals when you're practically living in your kitchen!

Rylon Recommendation We *strongly* encourage you to take out zero-deductible insurance on the campervan you rent. Your travel insurance, your at-home auto insurance, and the auto insurance tied to your credit cards may or may not cover campervans or RVs, so check your policies carefully. Even if they do cover you for regular collision, it's not likely to be as good a deal as the zero-deductible plans available directly from the rental agency. In fact, the price I've quoted for our campervan rental included the maximum insurance package. Good thing, since we actually needed it. Let's just say someone took one of the very sharp turns into the back section of a campsite a little too close, tapping a big-ass rock with the side of the van, which led to a leaky gray water pipe.

Knowing that we had no obligation for that slight oopsy or any more serious ones that might have occurred saved us a lot of stress. After all, you're on vacation. The last thing you want to have to worry about is piloting an oversized van through tight quarters (still on the "wrong" side of the road, mind you) when you're used to puttering around your hometown in a tiny convertible that doesn't even have a backseat. Just saying.

I was also extremely pleased with the company we used to rent our campervan. Maui (www.maui-rentals.com/nz/en) was competitive price-wise, had shuttle buses, their office is close to the international airport in Auckland, and their check-in and check-out processes were speedy and efficient. The models they had available to choose from would suit anyone from a solo traveler to a couple like us or even a full family. A staff member took the time to walk through the vehicle with us and make sure we understood all its features and were comfortable before turning us loose.

We had booked our campervan far in advance as is recommended, especially if you're traveling during New Zealand's peak summer season from December to February. However, that doesn't mean you have to miss out on deals. The company graciously price-matched a significant discount they offered months later. So be sure to look for coupons when booking and check frequently after that for sales you can apply to your rental. Part of the reason they allow this is because they have an excellent cancellation policy, which would allow you to cancel and rebook under the sale if they didn't price match. For cancellations more than three months in advance there is no fee at all, and subsequent cancellations have a sliding scale fee. Even up to 24 hours before the rental period, they only charge half the rental fee. I think this is extremely fair given the low cost and the fact that cancelling that late means you probably had an emergency situation. And that's why you have trip insurance, right? Right.

Knowing all this, I was happy to make my reservation nearly a year in advance, though I'm sure you don't need to do it quite that early to get what you want.

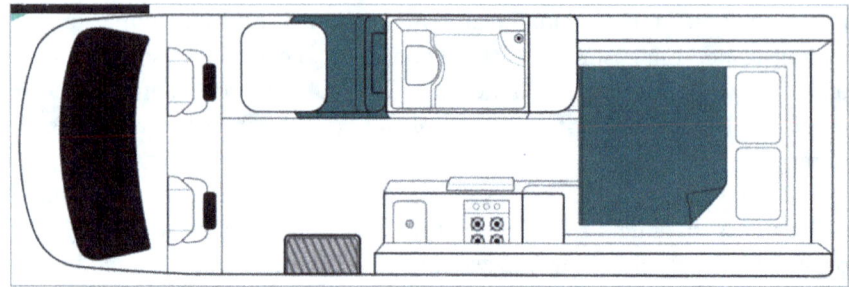

Diagram from http://www.maui-rentals.com/nz/en/motorhome-hire/2-berth-campervan-ultima

A little about our campervan... We rented the two-berth Ultima. When you're not actively traveling, the front seats swivel 180 degrees to make a little living room area including a table between them and the bench immediately behind them. In the middle of the van, there is a small but functional bathroom and kitchen. At the rear, a spacious bed can also be converted to a table and couches during the day. Given the forward seating, we opted to leave the bed in this configuration all the time, which also gave us more room to store our luggage under it. There is also a handy storage area accessed from the rear of the van. The van has a TV and microwave as well as all the necessities to cook in the kitchen. Onboard WiFi was an option as well, but we elected to rely on our cellular service through the SIM card we'd picked up at the airport. Coverage was decent, though there were a few more remote spots in deep gorges where we had to actually talk to each other instead of surfing the web. Eek!

Most important to note, the Ultima is a self-contained van. This means it has a bathroom and a black water tank for storing poop. There, I said it. This is important because you'll find that a lot of campsites, especially free campsites, require that your vehicle be self-contained in order for you to stay there. Nobody wants people leaving "presents" on their private land or in their public parks. Also, because New Zealand does have this strong campervan movement, there have—unfortunately—been people who have abused the system. Therefore, be sure to always look for signs that say freedom camping is permitted when you pick a place to park overnight. Otherwise, an instant fine can be assessed.

Here's probably a good place to tell you about the most important tool you'll need to make van life smooth sailing. The Campermate (www.campermate.co.nz) app is invaluable. It's a crowd-sourced database of points of interest, bathrooms, dump sites, campsites, facilities, grocery stores,

WiFi hotspots, gas stations, and more. Anything you need to know about, people have noted it in the app. Want to read reviews of a place you're thinking of staying at overnight? No problem. Just realized you're low on water and need to top up? No problem. Seriously, this thing is pure gold and it's free.

All in all, we never once had a problem finding premium spots to park and stay overnight. *When* we go back to New Zealand (not if), we will definitely be rejoining the campervan crowd.

After some coffee and refreshments, a giant pile of free maps and coupons, a van tour, and some basic information about what we'd gotten ourselves into, we were unleashed on New Zealand in our spiffy campervan. The first thing we did, of course, was drive to the nearest grocery store and stock up on supplies.

The Countdown Auckland Airport location is just three kilometers from the Maui rental office and is an easy maiden voyage to take in your campervan to get settled in. The parking lot is accessed through wide roads and has special larger spots for campervans in the back. I have a feeling we're not the first people to have this genius idea!

It was another huge benefit to van life. Just like staying in apartments in Australia, having cooking facilities and our own food onboard allowed us to save money on breakfast, drinks, and snacks. We reserved our meal budget for a few fancy indulgences along the way that I'll of course tell you more about later. Also, because we took our house with us everywhere, we were able to pause whatever we were doing to eat lunch in the campervan without having to waste time backtracking to an apartment or hotel. That definitely saved us some money.

We'd make sandwiches and eat in our camper or outside it in really amazing locations with awesome views at premium attractions. The campervan even came with an external grill that folded out so we could cook outside, and an optional awning and chairs to expand our living space. We didn't get to take advantage of those features because it was still pretty dang cold when we visited, but we definitely would have if the weather had been nicer.

With that said, don't be afraid to stay in a campervan in cool weather. I'm not talking "arctic wind, South Island in prime ski season" weather, although you might be okay there, too, but the temperatures were in the forties every night we stayed in New Zealand and we were fine. The campervan came with plenty of blankets and a small electric heater, which we used when we had mains power at a campsite. It also had a diesel heater, which we used only once or twice to get the warmth jumpstarted on the coldest evenings. The heater uses fuel from the van's regular gas tank. It shuts off when you have a certain amount of diesel left so that you aren't in danger of stranding yourself if you fall asleep with it on. That's another feature I'd make sure the campervan had if I did this again in the future.

So once you've loaded up on groceries (hopefully things like paper plates and canned or microwavable food, which will make your life easier) I'd take as much time as you need here to stow everything in as efficient a manner as possible. Shove your suitcases far under the bed, put your clothes (hopefully in packing cubes) in the overhead bins. Arrange supplies in a way that you can easily reach the things you need the most.

Don't let my glowing review make you think a campervan is the same thing as a ginormous Class A big rig. It's not. But by making every inch count, it can be very comfortable, fun, and extra cozy.

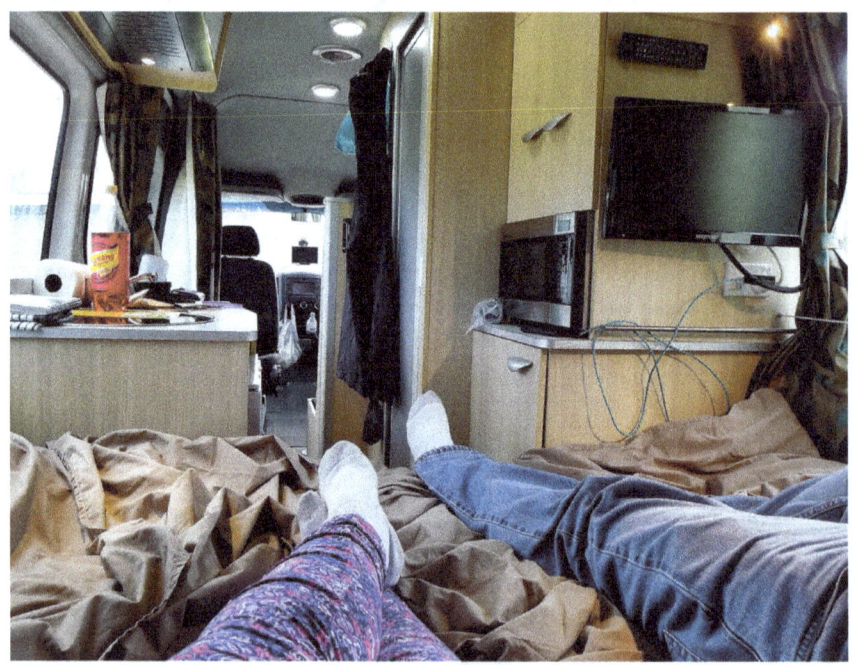

Home sweet campervan. The kitchen is to the left and the bathroom to the right in this photo.

Once we were stocked up and had worked up our nerve, we pulled out of the grocery store parking lot and headed for our first destination, the glowworm caves (www.waitomo.com) in Waitomo! The drive itself wasn't particularly difficult. There wasn't too much traffic and it only took about two and a half hours to travel the 185 kilometers to the visitor center. The area around the cave is gorgeous, filled with rolling green hills dotted with cows and lambs.

At the caves themselves, soaring steam-bent beams laced with canvas tarps make an outdoor shelter that covers a dining area, spotless public bathrooms, a theater that plays a short movie about the area and its people for context, an exhibition hall, and a gift shop, along with the ticket booths for the various tours.

Although you can also go black water rafting or visit three different cave systems (including one that is entirely wheelchair accessible), the most popular tour is for the glowworm cave. It leaves no less than every 30 minutes between 9 a.m. and 5 p.m., and lasts for about 45 minutes. An adult ticket costs $31.95 and is worth every penny.

You pass through a lush forest before entering into a crack in the side of the mountain. After checking out some large cavern spaces that are impressive in their own right, you wander down toward the bank of a subterranean river. By now, your eyes will have begun to adjust to the dim lighting and you might spot dots of luminescence on the limestone walls or ceiling.

These are glowworms, *Arachnocampa luminosa* to be exact. What looks like a romantic twinkle of living blue stars in a false night sky is really more like zillions of gnat larvae trying to lure food into their goopy traps, but hey, stick with the twinkling stars if it makes you feel better about going to gawk at bug nests as you glide underneath them in a small wooden boat propelled through absolute darkness with only their ethereal light to guide you.

All kidding aside, it really is spectacular and only slightly creepy.

This is one of those places you may have seen in jaw-dropping Instagram images or those "wonders of the world" articles that float around Facebook from time to time. I would love to plop a picture in here of the otherworldly blue streaks dripping from the cave ceiling above the still, inky water, but cameras are not allowed on this tour. To be honest, I don't think regular gear or a cell phone would do it justice anyway, as it's a very low light situation.

You'll just have to go see it for yourself or check out their website, which has some pretty representative images of what is waiting for you in Waitomo.

After we'd spent the afternoon here, we were ready to settle in. We'd debated poking around the Campermate app for a freedom camping site in the area to take advantage of surrounding ourselves in the gorgeous landscape. However, on our way in, we passed the Top 10 Waitomo Holiday Park (www.waitomopark.co.nz) just down the road. It seemed like the simple, easy, and inexpensive alternative for our first night in the campervan, so we pulled in to ask if they had vacancies. They did, and we nabbed a spot for $35.05. If you don't have a campervan to sleep in, they also have cabins for rent.

Again, we had the luxury of spontaneity because we were there in the shoulder season. If you're traveling at peak times, I'm sure this place would be booked solid well in advance because it offers a lot of amenities close to the main attraction in the area. There was a pool and hot tub as well as a playground for kids. Each space had electricity and water hookups. A communal kitchen, library, and TV room was also available for guest usage. The shower and bathroom facilities were clean and brightly lit, even at night.

Even better, the park is adjacent to a restaurant that I had on my list of potential places to try out. Huhu (www.huhucafe.co.nz) is one place you don't want to miss, whether or not you stay at the Top 10 Holiday Park. This café is perched on the hill above the park and is made almost entirely of glass. The view is surpassed only by the food, which was both incredible and affordable. We stuffed ourselves on lamb, king salmon, and a few drinks but still managed to keep the bill under $50 for two people.

They even took the time to concoct some sort of steaming hot, extremely potent ginger drink that cut right through my congestion when they realized I was sick. Someday I'll have to go back for the ice cream sundae with homemade marshmallows, which also looked divine.

After dinner, we went back to the van to snuggle in for the night. If I'd been feeling better, we might have checked out the Ruakuri Bush Walk off of Tumutumu Road, where I was told you can see even more glowworms for free and try to snap some pictures of them. Be sure to take a flashlight if you attempt this after dark.

There are several other hikes and outdoor attractions including Marokopa Falls, the Mangapohue Natural Bridge, and the Timber Trail with a spectacular suspension bridge for cyclists if you'd like to spend more time in this area before moving on.

But for us, the next day was going to be for exploring a new stop on our tour.

DAY 13 - TAUPO

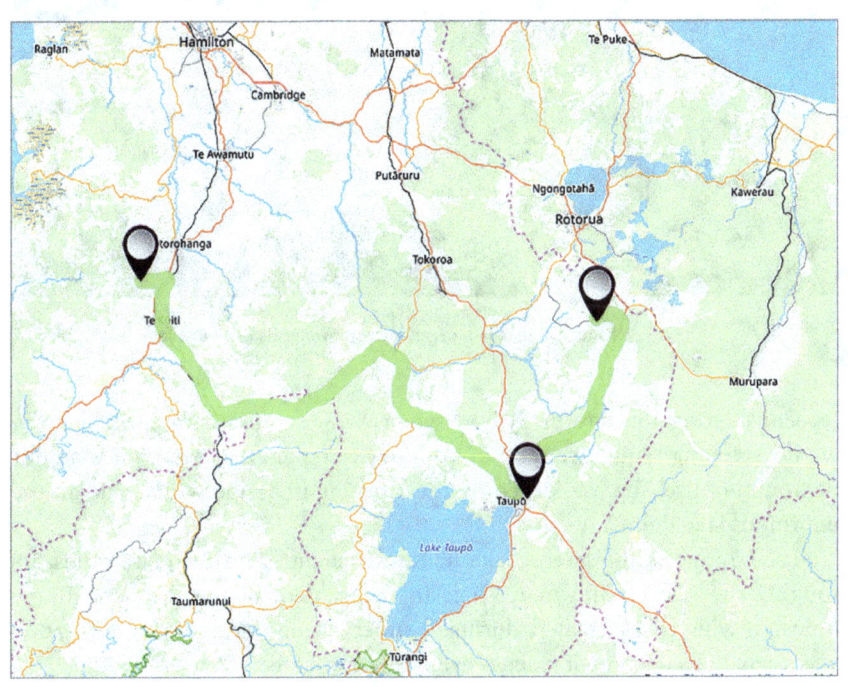

© OpenStreetMap contributors

This day began with another early morning, but one that was well worth it. The drive between Waitomo and Taupo is only about 150 kilometers long. Still, it can be slow going because you're driving a big vehicle on squiggly roads, and there are things—like herds of sheep, or lumber-cutting projects—that can sometimes block the way. It's also a very beautiful drive, filled with a thousand shades of green, so you may find you want to pull over to take pictures or let the driver enjoy the view for a few minutes as well. Budget some extra time and you won't regret it...or miss your boat.

Around each curve in the road was another sprawling vista like this one.

Considering the day in Sydney when we were forced to sprint for the whale watching cruise, we were in no hurry to repeat that experience on our next mini-cruise. Yep, we kicked off the morning in Taupo with a ride on the enormous lake there.

Lake Taupo is the largest lake in New Zealand. At 238 square miles, it's roughly the size of Singapore! It is in the caldera of the dormant Taupo Volcano, which was created during a supervolcanic eruption about 27,000 years ago. At its deepest, it reaches over six hundred feet.

It seems there are about a half dozen tour operators willing to take you out for a spin on the water, and they all make a trip out to the dominant point of interest on the lake in the late morning each day. However, there is a lot of variety between them. For example, there is a kayak option and a steamboat option. You can sail out there on a small monohull with the wind in your face, or you can ride in comfort on an enclosed boat with food and included WiFi.

I'm not ashamed to admit that's the option we chose. We went with Chris Jolly Tours (https://chrisjolly.co.nz). We did this predominantly because we didn't have the time it would take to go on one of the slower methods of transportation, though I would have really liked to sail out there myself. The boat left at 10:30 a.m. and the tour lasted approximately 90 minutes.

For $32.20 per person, this was a pretty decent deal as it also included refreshments like coffee, tea, and muffins. I enjoyed the extensive history of the area that was shared by the captain as well as an onboard documentary of the region that played while we made our way to the western side of the lake. If that's not your thing, there is of course free WiFi to entertain yourself with as well. Because I'd stopped at the Spark kiosk on arrival in New Zealand, we had internet access through my phone which I hot-spotted to Mr. Rylon. If you didn't have that, this would be a good chance to check your emails quickly while you're waiting to depart or send your mom a message to let her know you hadn't been pecked to death by a giant kiwi or something equally preposterous since I'm guessing my mom isn't the only one able to imagine horrible things when their child is on the other side of the earth and doesn't check in once in a while, right?

Anyway, I wouldn't want to be fiddling with my phone for the entire trip, however, because it was very beautiful. The mountains surrounding the serene lake will have you reaching for your camera.

After you've learned a bit about the Taupo area, you glide up to a cliff wall where traditional Maori imagery was carved into the stone in the late 1970s by Matahi Whakataka-Brightwell and John Randall in the belief that the traditional symbolism will protect the lake from future volcanic activity. The thirty-foot-tall carvings are as interesting as the legends behind the symbolism included in the portrait of Ngatoroirangi, an ancient navigator who led the Tuwharetoa and Te Arawa tribes to the area more than a thousand years ago.

Some of the carvings at Lake Taupo.

Once back to shore, it was about lunchtime. If you walk a few blocks up from the marina, where there was plenty of parking for campervans by the way, you'll find an assortment of great shops and restaurants to try out. The town of Taupo itself has a relaxed resort feel like many similar getaways in the US. There are no tall buildings or bustling traffic to mar the views or tranquility of being around the water.

Mr. Rylon and I chose the Spoon and Paddle (www.facebook.com/spoonandpaddle) to duck into. The artisan flair to the food here turned simple pleasures into something special. I had the lamb shank and risotto, but it was presented with pea vines and some sort of crispy, crackery goodness that made it far different than anything I've ever pulled out of a slow cooker in my own kitchen.

Lamb shank and risotto at the Spoon and Paddle gets two thumbs up!

After lunch, we decided it was time to move on, especially because I wanted to make one more stop along the way and I wasn't quite sure how long it would take. If you come this close, I would definitely not pass up Huka Falls (www.hukafalls.com). It was less than a ten-minute drive from Taupo and well worth a peek, even if you don't get out and walk around. Although if you have the chance, I would do that, too.

These falls are very unusual because of the sheer volume of water that passes over them. Sure, I've seen waterfalls that are much taller or maybe even more picturesque. But even compared to Niagara Falls' Horseshoe Falls, which always impress me with their force, this waterfall almost made me nervous to be around. It is loud and unbelievably powerful due to the narrowing of the river that feeds it as it forces its way through a skinny gorge. In stark contrast to the peaceful lake, this water is angry and churns as it slams through the gorge and into the pool below.

You can walk a short way from the parking lot over a bridge where you see the water picking up speed as it rushes along a sloped bed toward the falls themselves. Even this spot makes you hope the bridge doesn't give out!

A bit farther on, there is an outlook for viewing the actual falls and the basin where the water smashes into the lake below. You can actually take a jet boat into this area and experience the falls from within that bubbling, foamy cauldron, but the viewing platform was plenty close enough for me.

Huka Falls is an eye-opening example of the power of nature.

I'm not trying to discourage you from seeing these falls for yourself—quite the opposite. They were a great reminder of how powerful the forces of nature can be and why they should be respected. There's another viewing area on the road above the falls that Mr. Rylon and I discovered by accident. It gave a different, but no less impressive perspective seeing the water racing through the gorge and gushing over the falls from higher up. So if this is your thing, you could easily spent hours hiking on trails surrounding this area.

Mr. Rylon and I had a much more relaxing plan for the remainder of the day, so we continued to our campground for the night, which was nestled in the Waikite Valley just 40 minutes away. Right before we got there, we stopped at a gas station along the road. I was surprised at first to see a sign warning people with allergies that there were a lot of bees around. Then I started seeing them buzzing everywhere, not bothering anyone.

That's because this place, and many others in this area, are known for beekeeping and—even better—making amazing honey. Check your local regulations on importing natural products like honey before purchasing more than you can consume during your trip. If you're allowed to bring it home, I think it makes an excellent souvenir for yourself or those you care about. The honey from this region is incredible. Many shops will know which packages can be brought into which countries, so ask. The flavors range from sage to blackberry, and I've been enjoying it my tea since we returned.

The reason we pulled into our campground earlier than usual was because Waikite Valley Thermal Pools (www.hotpools.co.nz) has a few bonus features that none of our other stopovers included. Namely, the hot springs!

They've taken natural geothermal springs and incorporated them into a series of cascading manmade pools integrated into the lush landscape of broad-leaved plants and exotic flowers. While we were here, there was an almost constant fog of steam rising from the verdant valley along with a lovely sulfur-y smell that Mr. Rylon assured me wasn't the result of him eating too many eggs for breakfast.

Okay, that part isn't the greatest, but hey...take the good with the not-as-good.

Honestly, the slight negative is nothing compared to how amazing this sight was. It's stunning and peaceful. Although there were other people around, it's not very big and—at least at the time of year we visited—never got crowded. The main pool looks like a regular swimming pool and most of the children were playing there.

In addition to that large area, there are several more secluded options, where most of the adults were tucked away in couples or small groups. The higher up the slope, the hotter the pools were, so you can either pick the temperature you prefer or pick the location you like best or just pick the place that's free of other guests.

If privacy is your main concern, there are even small cabins you can rent. Each has its own isolated pool that can only be used by the person occupying the cabin. Since by chance we had a pool to ourselves anyway, it didn't seem like a worthwhile upgrade on the day we visited.

The pools themselves are made of charcoal-colored stone and are of varying depths. It was very comfortable to sit and read on my Kindle while listening to the sheep in the distance with rejuvenating steam rising all around. I credit some serious soaking here along with my antibiotics for helping me kick that damn chest infection.

The thermal pools at Waikite Valley could entice you to spend your whole vacation floating in them.

If you did get too hot, you could stand up and walk around in the pool or move to a shallower spot for a while. With the cool September air, in the fifties at its highest that day, we were comfortable enough for an extended stay.

The main lodge here has a café where we had some pretty excellent fish and chips. There is also a selection of beer, ice cream, and other snacks. You can use the pools at this facility even if you aren't camping here for a fee of $18.36 per person per day, but if you rent a campsite for $36.64 a night, your entrance fee to the pools is included in the price. We found this to be an excellent value and I wouldn't hesitate to return here. It was a magical experience and one I will always remember.

One thing to note, due to the extremely steep sides of the gorge this campground is located in, they do not offer WiFi and my cellular internet and phone service didn't reach us. So this is truly off the grid, which is a nice break and gave me an excuse not to do any work during our stay.

Of course, in case of emergency, it's not that far to the top of the ridge, so a few minutes' drive would get you somewhere you could be connected to the rest of the world again. But why would you want to be?

DAY 14 - GEOTHERMAL WONDERLAND AND ROTORUA

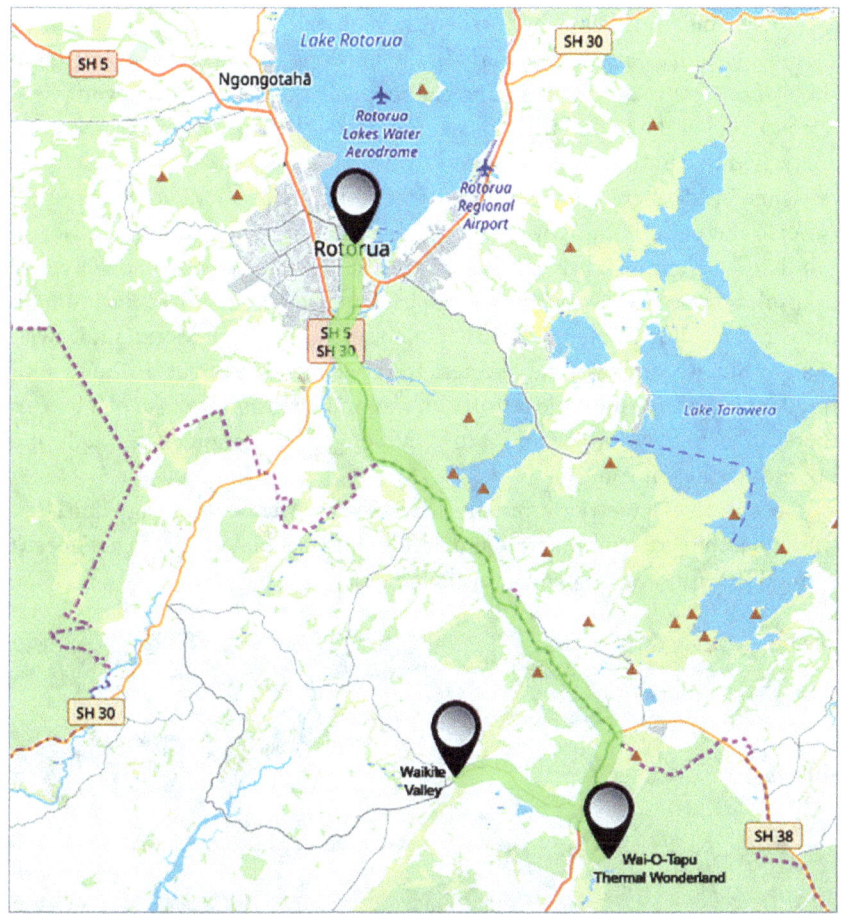

© OpenStreetMap contributors

This was one of my favorite days. Okay, I realize I've said that a bunch already. But seriously. This was a fantastic place overflowing with activities and sights worth seeing. If I was planning the itinerary again I'd be tempted to stay here longer, except I don't know where I'd steal the time from as there really wasn't anything we did or anywhere we went that I didn't enjoy.

So I guess you just need a full three weeks or more for this vacation

It's a quick ten-minute drive from the Waikite Valley to Wai-O-Tapu Geothermal Wonderland (www.waiotapu.co.nz). This is an 18-square-kilometer geothermal park featuring geysers, colorful thermal pools, and boiling mud springs. It opens at 8:30 a.m.

I'd recommend being there when they unlock the gates for a couple of reasons. First, it's not crowded early in the morning so you can get some great shots of the features without a bunch of people in them, obstructing your view. Second, one of the main attractions at the park—the Lady Knox Geyser show—is scheduled for 10:15 every morning.

Once inside there are three options for trails—1.5, 2, or 3 kilometers—that traverse the park. I admit, we kind of went through this area quickly. Not so fast that I don't think it was worth the $22.10 admission fee per person, because it absolutely was. We saw the most spectacular of the features, including a neon green sulfuric pool that would put a radioactive vat of Mountain Dew to shame. But we did take the shortest trail, which took about an hour with frequent stops to admire the rainbow of mineral deposits and take pictures, so there is definitely opportunity to stay longer and wander through the boardwalks here if you like.

Be sure to stay strictly on the marked pathway so that you don't fall through a thin crust of minerals and accidentally get boiled alive. That doesn't sound like a fun way to spend a vacation day!

Beautiful and dangerous, geothermal activity makes for some breathtaking landscapes.

The reason we opted for the shortest path through the park was because every morning at precisely 10:15, they set off their geyser. It's a short drive away from the main visitor center, so keep that in mind when you're planning out your time. Either get your tickets when you enter or be sure to leave a few minutes to do that at the gift shop before making the quick trip over to the viewing arena. There is about a half-hour informational show given by one of the rangers, which was pretty interesting, before the geyser blows. After you've been educated, the ranger pours biodegradable soap into the geyser to reduce the surface tension and set the geyser off.

It's a fantastic photo opportunity, and you just might learn something, too.

The geyser would naturally erupt every few days, though unpredictably, without intervention from the ranger, so this felt like a good compromise between something artificial and making sure you get to see the good stuff.

Rylon Recommendation Despite a sign at the entrance to Geothermal Wonderland that says there are additional bathrooms in the park, we never saw them. So make sure you take advantage of the ones in the visitor center, or your campervan facilities, before you walk out into the fields of boiling sulfuric mud because no one wants to have to pop a squat in the bushes and burn something important off, okay?

After the geyser show, we climbed back into our trusty house-on-wheels and headed for Rotorua. Another reason we explored Wai-o-tapu before the geyser show and not after was because I'd booked a Segway tour of Rotorua (www.rotoruabysegway.com), which started at 1:30 p.m.

Since the geyser show wrapped up around 10:45 and it's only a 25-minute drive to downtown Rotorua, we ended up having more than two hours to spare once we arrived. So if there's something you didn't manage to see before the geyser show, you have a chance to take another look after before moving on.

Mr. Rylon and I used our free time to have lunch at Urbano Bistro (www.urbanobistro.co.nz), which is where the Segway tour departs from anyway. Fortunately, they had superb food as well. I got fried mac and cheese and Mr. Rylon had the big boy breakfast. They weren't lying. The portions were enormous, so you could definitely share an entrée. Aside from that, the dishes had a gourmet flair that elevated them above standard diner fare. Don't forget to try the desserts, which were also excellent here. All in, we spent $49.01 for lunch and treats.

Once we finished eating, we still had some time to kill, so we digested in the comfort of the campervan, which was parked on the street outside. A serious perk of this kind of travel. You can be comfortable even during the day when you have a couple minutes to relax and rest.

So...the Segway tour. What is it?

A Segway is a two-wheeled electric personal transportation device that self-balances. If you've never ridden one before, don't worry! Mr. Rylon hadn't either. Other than a few basic requirements, like being able to stand for the duration of your tour, and a weight restriction of about 260lbs (it varies by tour operator and Segway model), there's nothing to it.

It's very intuitive even for someone clumsy like me. The machine does all of the work for you. All you have to do is lean in the direction you want to go and it will take you there. I will warn you, the first moment you step on the Segway is going to be a doozy. It was for me, and has been for every other person I've watched do it. The gyroscope in the machine compensates for your angle and tries to right you no matter what you do. At first, human nature will have you try to keep your balance for the machine (like you would on a bike). So almost everyone wobbles to and fro for a couple of seconds before stabilizing themselves.

It was at that precise moment on my maiden voyage on a Segway that I thought, oh hell no. This is not for me. But it was! Don't give up. Each Segway tour I've been on allows about ten to fifteen minutes at the beginning of the tour to acclimate you to the device, usually in an empty parking lot. After that, I promise you'll be comfortable and ready to go, wondering why you were worried about it in the first place.

To operate the Segway, all you do is angle your body—forward to go, back to stop, left and right to steer or turn. It's like gliding over the pavement and, frankly, a total blast. It also happens to be an incredible way to see a city. I've done this in Columbus, OH, where I live, as well as in Rotorua, and I'll be signing up for more of these wherever I have the option.

Dorky? Maybe. But also tons of fun.

We went about twelve kilometers in two and a half hours, stopping frequently to enjoy the sights and learn more about them. That's more ground than we could have covered in a traditional walking tour and yet we saw a lot more things up close than we would have been able to in a bus tour. It's a great compromise.

Plus you look super cool in your helmet and booger-colored reflective vest, yeah!

One of the key sights on the tour was Kuirau Park. It's a well-maintained city greenspace that happens to be dotted with more geothermal features that lend it an alien flair. Of course, the acidic gas from these fumaroles sent me into a coughing fit (refer back to my crazy respiratory infection during this part of the trip). Our tour guide was gracious enough to pull over at a picnic table. He then zipped off to get me some water and cough drops from a convenience store on our route so I didn't die and could thoroughly enjoy the rest of our ride. Mr. Rylon and I were the only people on our tour. It was tailored to us and personalized with our interests in mind. For that reason in addition to the fun factor of riding the Segways, I felt the $101.42 for this tour was money well spent.

It was while standing in the grass, absolutely not on or touching the

Segway, that I managed to bend my fingernail completely backwards against my cell phone while trying to simultaneously take a picture and not suffocate from the combination of the fumes and my illness.

I'm sharing my embarrassing moment for a couple of reasons.

1. Riding a Segway is easy and not dangerous. I know this for a fact because our tour guide had NEVER used his first aid kit before the bloody mess I made of my thumb. In fact, he wasn't even sure what was inside it, having never opened the thing before. He first withdrew an ACE bandage, which I discouraged him from using until we could rummage up a Band-Aid from the depths of the plastic box. This held my thumbnail mostly together until Mr. Rylon and I could perform surgery on it in the campervan later. But that's a story for another time.

2. Even when things don't go perfectly, they're still worth doing. Don't let fear or self-consciousness stop you from trying something new on vacation (or ever in life, I suppose) because it all worked out fine in the end. I hopped back on the Segway, finished out the tour, and we had an awesome time. Besides, I'm pretty sure that tour guide will never forget me!

Other highlights of the tour, which I'd suggest checking out no matter how you get there, were the Te Papaiouru Marae (an example of a meeting place for Māori people blanketed in carvings you can read more about here: www.newzealand.com/us/feature/marae-maori-meeting-grounds), the boardwalk at Lake Rotorua, and Government Gardens.

The Rotorua Museum was closed due to earthquake damage when we were there but the exterior was still worth seeing!

The large, elaborate building at the center of Government Gardens is the Rotorua Museum (www.rotoruamuseum.co.nz/visit-us/government-gardens). You should verify online if it's open to the public because it was damaged in an earthquake a few months before we visited. Until the building can be repaired, it's closed. Still, there is plenty to see in the surrounding gardens and bathhouse. We even got to watch some of a lawn bowling match in progress.

After our tour, we checked in to the Rotorua Top 10 Holiday Park (www.rotoruatop10.co.nz), which cost $40.22 for the night. The hairpin entrance here would be tricky with anything larger than the campervan we had, but the facilities were as nice as the affiliated place we'd stayed in Waitomo. They included a pool, a hot tub filled with mineral water, a play area with a giant inflatable trampoline for kids, a laundromat, and a decent kitchen area. The shower areas were roomy, clean, and even heated!

While here we mastered the art of opening a can of SpaghettiOs for dinner without a functioning can opener, since the kitchen on site has the facilities to cook but absolutely no supplies. We also discovered that it's possible to turn on the water in the Ultima's sink while the lid of the sink is closed so that water pours all over the floor. You know, van life stuff that was all part of the adventure.

The good thing about having a space at a campground versus a freedom camping spot is that you can come and go as you please without worrying about losing your parking place. This was especially important as, despite the day chock full of amazing things we'd already done, there was one more activity on my itinerary for Rotorua.

We waited for sunset, then set off for the nearby Redwoods Treewalk (www.treewalk.co.nz/en_US). If you are afraid of heights or things that sway when you walk on them, this is probably not the activity for you. For everyone else...oh yeah. Go for it.

After buying tickets, which you can do at the base of the giant redwood tree where the walk starts, you climb up a spiral wooden staircase to about twenty feet into the actual canopy. Well, "canopy" might be pushing it, as these century-old trees are hundreds of feet tall and you're not *that* far off the ground. But it feels like it. Especially if you choose to do this at night.

One of the ticket options is to buy a day and night pass. The daytime- or nighttime-only ticket is $19.72 and the combo ticket is $26.52. If we'd had a chance to do this again in daylight, I would have grabbed that opportunity. We enjoyed this so much I would have liked to do it again when we could get a different perspective. However, if I could only choose one option, I'm glad we got to visit at night.

After dusk, the forest is illuminated with giant paper lanterns and colored lights. I felt like I was walking through an enchanted elven fairytale forest. Then again, we weren't all that far from Hobbiton, which was on the agenda for first thing the next morning.

After climbing to the first station—part treehouse, part lookout platform that rings the redwood tree in an eco-friendly design—we could see a suspension bridge leading from it across the parking lot to more redwoods in the distance.

The first suspension bridge at the Redwoods Treewalk leads over the parking lot and into the forest beyond.

Here's where you need to be brave or fake it. The thirty or so suspension bridges are sturdy, but they do sway as you walk on them. There are rope handholds and it's steady enough that even people who aren't regular adventure seekers will have no trouble with the actual physical requirements at this park. However, there is a squirminess factor in traversing the space between the trees on moving bridges, especially if your husband is like mine and bounces around on the bridge while you're on it just to freak you out.

All in good fun, though, since I'm not particularly afraid of heights and it was clear that the attraction was well maintained. Everything here is fairly new. In fact, just this year they added a section of walkway that is included in the ticket price yet optional to visit. It is sixty feet off the ground.

This was a fantastic place for an evening stroll. As you progress deeper into the woods, the colorful lights and lanterns make it seem like you are truly in some forest king's grand hall. For more practical-minded visitors, informational signs posted at every major tree along the way ensure you learn about the environment as you go.

In between each bridge is a firm platform where you can admire the views or catch your breath on built-in benches. You can sit for a while to take in the forest, lamps, and colors painting the forest around you for a while before proceeding to the next bridge.

The system of bridges and platforms work their way higher to a maximum of about forty feet off the ground as you go until you reach the halfway point of the trip. This is also where you can access the new, high section if you dare. From there, the walkway starts to gradually descend again in a wide oval that leads you back to the start.

The bathroom facilities were also pretty decent here for a treewalk in the middle of nowhere, so long as you make sure to avail yourself of them before climbing up to the bridges. From there you're stuck until you get back down.

Although we had our faithful campervan with us, we had at this point decided that the bathroom in it was better suited for emergencies than using it when there was a perfectly good alternative on hand because neither Mr. Rylon nor I was excited about the prospect of emptying the cassette toilet.

This is probably a good time to mention another option Maui offers with campervan rental—their express return package. If you buy this, you don't have to refill the propane for the stove, empty the toilet cassette, or refill the gas tank before bringing the campervan back. You basically just toss them the keys and leave. Mr. Rylon and I agreed it was worth $225 to avoid all that hassle. It would also be a good place to shave a little off your expenses if you don't mind doing those things yourself.

With that, our time here was up.

You could easily spend an entire week exclusively in Rotorua if you wanted to. In addition to all the things we got to experience, there is a wildlife park, a 3D trick art gallery, a bird of prey center, stand-up paddleboarding, a living reenactment of an ancient Māori village, a giant hedge maze, horseback riding, lake activities, escape rooms, spas, wineries, a gondola, luging, and so much more to keep you and your travel buddies of all ages entertained.

No trip to the North Island is complete without a visit to Rotorua.

DAY 15 - MATAMATA AND TAURANGA

© OpenStreetMap contributors

Next stop, Hobbiton (www.hobbitontours.com)! Yes, I know it sounds cheesy. But I'm an author, *The Lord of the Rings* was my favorite book growing up, and our cats' names are Bilbo and Frodo. There was no way in hell I was going all the way to New Zealand and *not* seeing the Party Tree with my own eyes. None.

If you have no clue what I'm talking about, *The Lord of the Rings* is an epic movie trilogy that was shot in New Zealand. The movie set for the main characters' hometown still exists near Matamata. After visiting Hobbiton, I can honestly say that even if you aren't a huge fan, this place is worth a peek. It's beautiful and you get lots of behind-the-scenes info on how a movie is made.

We debated driving out to Matamata from Rotorua the night before. A freedom camping spot somewhere in the area would have been nice because it's pretty remote and we had tickets for the very first tour of the day. Then again, we went to the nighttime tree walk the evening before and didn't particularly want to drive on rural roads in the dark.

The tipping point was that we just happened to visit Hobbiton on International Hobbit Day, so we knew the place would be packed. Therefore, we opted to stay in Rotorua then get up early to make the hour-long trek over to Matamata. Honestly, after being out late at the redwoods park, I'm glad we stayed there and got some sleep. I'm extra glad we didn't skip the tree walk entirely to move on.

In reality, nothing is very far apart in New Zealand. That makes the trip even more exciting. There's a lot of doing and minimal traveling in between. But what traveling there is, is breathtaking. Be prepared to see greenery, sheep, and cows everywhere. Sort of like Ireland, but on the opposite side of the world, at least along the route we traveled. The country also has incredible diversity. Seaside towns, mountains, rolling farmlands, and geothermal areas—we saw them all in our circuit. If you added some of the far north areas or the South Island, the range of ecosystems would be even more impressive.

Once at Hobbiton, you board a bus for a short drive into the private areas of the movie set. This is still today an active sheep farm. Everything here is immaculately landscaped and maintained. You can pose by hobbit holes, learn how different-sized sets were used to make certain characters look taller or shorter than they are with forced perspective, and generally admire what is now a blossoming hillside garden.

Hobbiton will bring your imagination to life.

After a stroll through the residential area of Hobbiton, you cross the bridge past the mill and ahead is the Green Dragon Inn. The best part about it is that it's a fully functioning tavern. Inside, you're treated to a complimentary beer (or non-alcoholic ginger beer if you're like me) and you have the option to purchase a snack as well. You can sip your drink by the roaring fire and admire the carvings and detail inside the structure, or you can wander around outside until you reconvene with your guide.

The tour here was $57.12. This lands on the pricier side of things. If you're a book nerd, like us, it's a must-do. Had we been here later in the day, and on a day that wasn't International Hobbit Day, I probably would have sprung for the evening banquet, which looks like three Thanksgiving feasts at once. A meal fit for a hobbit (or an author)!

After Hobbiton, our plan was to head to Tauranga for a helicopter tour over the coastal city. Given Mr. Rylon's fear of flying, this was a huge deal for him. Truth be told, I was pretty nervous about, it too. One of the very few regrets I have about my previous roaming is that the two times I've been to Hawaii, I wasn't able to do a helicopter tour there. That's partially because we were SCUBA diving on that trip so you can't fly within 24 hours of diving, partially because we didn't have enough time to fit it in, and mostly because I had to work up the nerve when I thought I'd have to do it alone.

So when I told Mr. Rylon I wanted to give it a whirl and he said he'd go, too, I booked a spot with Aerius Helicopters (www.aerius.co.nz) right away before either of us could wise up and change our minds. At $153.56 per person for a 20-minute ride over the bay and Mount Maunganui, this is for sure a luxury excursion rather than a must-have. I wish I could tell you it was extraordinary (and I'm sure it is), but we didn't get to fly so I can't say so from my own experience.

What happened? No, we didn't have a panic attack or bail at the last minute.

Mother Nature didn't cooperate. It had been drizzling and gray all day. We did still drive the hour to Tauranga. However, when we arrived it was pouring rain. I called the tour operator, and they were quick to confirm that it wouldn't be safe to fly that day or good viewing even if we had gone up. They refunded us promptly. I respect that they didn't go ahead with a subpar or dangerous outing just to make a buck or three hundred. If I could do it again, I would certainly hire them.

So, we pulled over on the side of the road and searched for a highly rated restaurant nearby where we could hunker down and enjoy a long lunch while the rain played itself out. While we were disappointed (and slightly relieved, I'm not going to lie), sometimes things like this turn into happy accidents, and this was definitely one of those times.

We found ourselves at Latitude 37 (www.latitude37restaurant.co.nz) and had what was easily one of the best meals of my life. The inside of the restaurant was perfect for the day, warm and welcoming with roaring fires, exposed brick, and raw wood everywhere. The food itself was classic and familiar with little twists here and there to make it more exciting. Quality was front and center, with top-notch ingredients shining through.

Mr. Rylon and I opted to go for a tapas-style meal and ordered a bunch of small plates to share. Scallops, lamb skewers, duck pate, and beef cheek sliders. We ate it all and loved every bite. I could eat here over and over yet never get tired of it. Especially since our haul cost just over $50.

While we ate, we discussed what to do next. Our original plan had been to do the helicopter tour and go out to a nice dinner, walk around the city, then move on the next morning to the Coromandel region on the far northeast coast. Since a lot of the attractions in this area are outdoor-based, like hiking the mountain or walking around the bay area, we decided to cut our losses and forge ahead.

This did mean another fairly long drive of about two and a half hours. That wouldn't ordinarily be an issue. Except if you zoom in on the map and check carefully, you'll see that this is one of the world's twistiest stretches of road.

Rylon Recommendation If you get carsick, or maybe even just a little green around the gills while driving, do yourself a favor and take Dramamine before you leave Tauranga. The road caught me completely by surprise. On the high-level map I looked at while route planning, it seemed relatively straight. That was complete and utter lies.

Since we've been on this trip, we've talked to several people who say this road is infamous for making people sick. Don't be one of them! Avoid motion sickness by taking medicine, stopping every half hour or so to recalibrate your equilibrium, and forsake looking through a camera or reading maps for too long while bouncing around curves in a campervan.

Trust me on this.

Though it was gorgeous, the drive from Tauranga to the campground near Hot Water Beach almost killed me. Probably in part due to all the rich food we'd just eaten and maybe because of the antibiotics I was on. I had to ask Mr. Rylon to pull over (which wasn't always possible on the steep hairpin turns) a half dozen times so that the world would stop spinning. Even still, by the time we ducked into the Top 10 Holiday Park (www.hotwaterbeachtop10.co.nz) in Hot Water Beach, I was wrecked.

Fortunately, they had space for us without a reservation. This place is in an ideal location relative to Hot Water Beach. It seems like it would be jam-packed in peak season, and the adorable non-traditional cabins here would be a blast to stay in if you didn't have a campervan. They are small buildings made of an arch of corrugated metal. Inside, gorgeous curved beams positioned like ribs hold up the structure and the layouts make the most of the modest spaces with a kitchen, bedroom, and living room in each. Some also have ensuite bathrooms. When I first saw them, the term glamping popped into my mind. However, this facility also offers an actual glamping option with beds inside roomy solar tents.

There's truly an option for everyone here. Prices range from about $18 for the backpacker lodge or an unpowered campsite to $200 for an ensuite or family-sized cabin. For our powered campsite, we paid $33.38.

I kicked Mr. Rylon out of the campervan because even his careful movements walking around the tiny space were making me sloshy inside. I promptly passed out while he enjoyed the fish and chips available for purchase in the park's takeout kiosk, and the TV in the extensive communal facilities, complete with a friendly resident cat. There were quite a few young couples here, not as many families with children. Had I been feeling better or the weather cooperated more during our two days here, I think we could have had a lot of fun meeting likeminded travelers.

DAY 16 - CATHEDRAL COVE, HOT WATER BEACH, AND WHITIANGA

The next morning I felt nearly human again. Unfortunately, the weather hadn't made as brilliant of a turnaround as I had. I bet in the summer, when the sky is blue and the sun is shining, this would be an incredibly scenic area. In warmer months, I suspect you could very happily pass days wandering up and down the coastline or lounging on the beach.

Unfortunately, it rained pretty much the entire time we were here, and it was the cold, unfriendly precipitation of early spring in that part of the world. While we visited, the high topped out around sixty degrees. That was great for walking around. Not good enough for swimming, snorkeling, or other activities that would really shine here.

Let's be honest, after two weeks on the go, it was kind of nice to have an excuse to be lazy and spend a long morning in the campervan. We cooked breakfast, looked out at the scenery, and read for a few hours instead of rushing around. The campground was sleepy and still. Very relaxing.

What I would have liked to try most—aside from sneaking in a SCUBA dive—was one of the kayaking trips to Cathedral Cove, a very famous natural archway along the coast. However, with both the rain and my chest infection just beginning to let up, we picked an alternative way of getting to this picturesque destination.

Glass Bottom Boat Whitianga (www.glassbottomboatwhitianga.co.nz) helped transform what could have been a bummer into a really memorable experience. We drove to the eastern side of Whitianga, then took a quick ferry across to the west side, saving a lot of driving around the inlet that bisects the town.

The two-hour tour costs $68 per person, but you're eligible for a 10% discount if you stay at the Top 10 Holiday Park. Our guide was hilarious, attentive, and knowledgeable. He also earned two thumbs up from Mr. Rylon for the way he put the pedal to the metal on the surprisingly zippy glass-bottomed boat we rode in. Again, probably due to the forecast and the time of year, there weren't many passengers onboard. It was just Mr. Rylon, me, and a young Japanese family of three on the tour.

I certainly wasn't complaining about that. We got to take our time, ask a lot of questions, and be sure that everyone captured as many memories as possible during the trip. We visited Champagne Bay, blowholes, sea caves, and pinnacles of rock that made impressive formations rising out of the sea. When the conditions are right you can also venture inside Orua Sea Cave, the third-largest sea cave in the Southern Hemisphere.

Cathedral Cove was awe inspiring. Check out how tiny those people on the beach look for a better idea of scale!

The sea life was pretty incredible as well. Starting with the big stuff, we saw New Zealand fur seals sunning themselves on the rocks. There's also a chance of spotting dolphins and even orcas in this area. Then they open up the viewing area of the bottom of the boat and suddenly you're invited into another world entirely, from the small things like urchins and sponges to schools of fish. It always amazes me when you see what's below the surface. In summer, you can also snorkel from this boat if you prefer to get a closer look.

Once we returned to Whitianga, we grabbed a quick bite to eat at the Harbour House Café directly across the street. The diner food here was better than I'd expected for an easy and inexpensive meal. The dessert selection was varied and tasty as well.

My intentions for the afternoon had been to check out the area's biggest draw, Hot Water Beach. It's an absolutely stunning stretch of sand bookended by magnificent cliffs. What makes it particularly special is the fact that the sand lies over a geothermal spring.

Be sure to check the tides and ask around to figure out the right time to enjoy this place while you're visiting. For about six hours each day, when the tide is low, you can rent a spade from any number of local places (or our campground had them on loan for free). Then you get to dig yourself a little spa right in the beach.

When I proposed this activity to Mr. Rylon, he did not share my enthusiasm. In fact, he thought I was joking and refused to get out of the campervan. He was entirely unimpressed with the idea of tromping around and digging a hole in the cold, wet sand for us to sit in and get rained on. As you might be sensing, this is the part of the trip where we'd both started to fade.

Between us, we were exhausted, sick, injured, and otherwise overwhelmed.

So although I was disappointed, I agreed we should skip it and regroup. I admit, as I watched everyone else heading down the road with their tiny shovels, I was extremely jealous. But sometimes you have to know your limits. Had we forced ourselves to power through that day in suboptimal conditions, I might not have been able to enjoy the rest of the trip.

Instead, we took a nap under our thick, puffy comforter with the sound of the rain pinging on our campervan roof and woke with big appetites.

Fortunately, there was a cute café we'd seen earlier called Hot Waves (www.facebook.com/Hot-Waves-Cafe-356915774325727) right up the street, so we decided to go check it out. I'm so glad we did! There was live folk music, local handcrafted souvenirs, wood-fired pizza, and even a pet cat. You could choose from regular tables or sofa seating, and the walls were covered in art for sale. The pizza was delicious and we enjoyed reading the regional newspapers as well.

It was the perfect end to another great day even if it didn't go according to plan.

Ones like these remind me that it's not always about fitting in as much as possible or knowing ahead of time what will be right for you on the day you're in a destination. So the more you can be flexible and enjoy whatever you stumble across, the more fun you'll have when roaming.

DAY 17 - THE LOST SPRING AND WHITIANGA TO TAKAPUNA

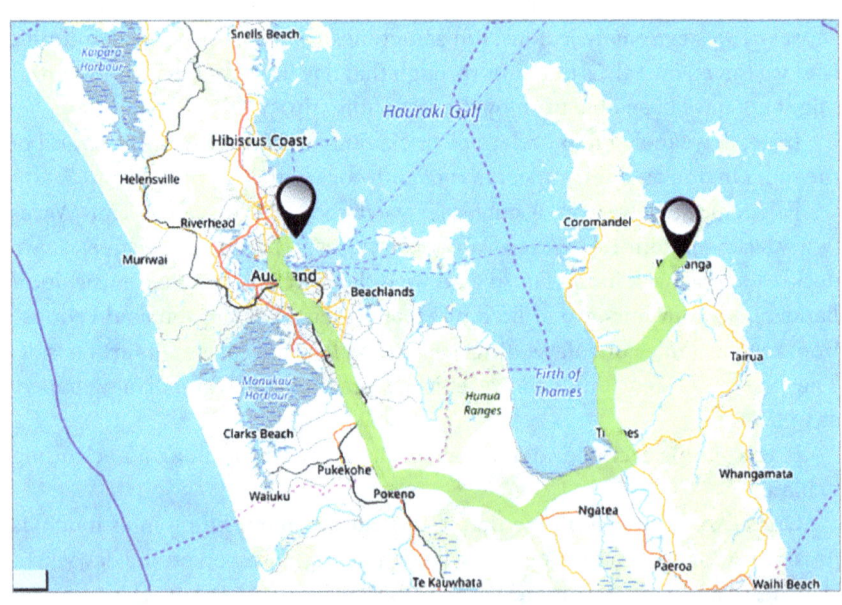

© OpenStreetMap contributors

I have a confession to make. When we left Columbus, OH at the start of our trip, I'd only finalized about 50% of my day-to-day detailed itinerary. I bought the in-flight WiFi and used it to book most of the activities we did in Australia. Then in the evenings while in Australia, I locked down tickets and reservations for a bunch of the attractions and campsites in New Zealand.

Due to a combination of running out of time and uncertainty, I left the tail end of the trip open for what we might discover we'd like to do along the way. I also took into account the probability that after three weeks in tiny spaces together, doing much more than we do at home, Mr. Rylon and I might be ready for a break—from vacation boot camp and maybe even from each other!

I'm happy to report that on this morning, I felt like a genius. Because as we'd been roaming around Whitianga the day before, we found the perfect thing to do for those final hours before we headed back to Auckland to wind down our vacation.

It came in the form of a very mysterious-sounding place that I honestly could live in, quite happily, for the rest of my life: the Lost Spring (www.thelostspring.co.nz). It's a day spa and geothermal pool system with a restaurant nestled in the heart of Whitianga. You can get an hour and a half pass to the springs for $27.20 or an all-day pass for $54.40 per person. They have various packages, including poolside food and beverage service or spa add-ons as well.

The plan was that we split up. I love swimming and warm water, so I brought my Kindle and was heading straight for the hot pools full of mineral-rich water from 2,200 feet below ground. Mr. Rylon planned to book himself a long massage, which he very much enjoys. He has a bad back, so given all the walking and adventuring we'd done, he was looking forward to that.

As an aside, the campervan bed was extremely spacious and comfortable for the both of us. It didn't bother Mr. Rylon's back at all. We even had plenty of room on the side to store my box of tissues when I couldn't breathe without them, our glasses, laptops, Kindles, phones, and whatever else we didn't feel like getting up to put away once we were sleepy without worry of rolling over and squishing things during the night.

Anyhoo, when we arrived, we learned that it's best to book any spa services well in advance, as the schedule was completely full for the day. Poor Mr. Rylon. Instead, he had to suffer and join me in the steamy, gorgeous pools. The landscaping at this place is incredible, including large rocks, sumptuous vegetation, and winding walkways that separate various nooks and crannies within the property. There was even a manmade crystal cave that was pretty fun to explore, if slightly cheesy since it was more fantastical than realistic. Birds zoomed in and out overhead, making it easy to imagine you were lost in the jungle somewhere instead of in the heart of a seaside town.

This is great because even though there were other people around, there were enough nooks and crannies that couples or friend groups could stay separate and feel nearly as private as if we had the place to ourselves.

I would gladly travel halfway around the world again for another day at The Lost Spring.

Another nice feature is that the pools are graded by temperature. The spa closest to where the water emerges from the bedrock below is hottest. It overflows from there, spreading out as it fills the rest of the system, and cooling as it goes. That's not to say the water is chilly at any point, because it's not. Even in the large, chest-deep main pool, we were toasty warm despite the early spring day.

Eventually, Mr. Rylon finally convinced me we had to get back on the road soon if we were going to make it to Auckland at a reasonable hour. I grudgingly dried off in the posh facilities and waved a sad goodbye to the outdoor areas of the Lost Spring. We were both essentially a pile of wet noodles at that point, so we sat down in their dining room to enjoy someone else making us lunch before we left.

To be honest, I felt like the meal was pricey for what we got and took quite a while to be served, but we had been spoiled by days and days of above-average culinary experiences on our journey. I got a lamb shank, which was good. Mr. Rylon had a steak and he also enjoyed it. Though perfectly satisfactory, neither was remarkable. In fact, I had to look back at my pictures to remember what I had there. We paid $60.54 for lunch including a few drinks. You could probably find something you'd enjoy more for less money in town—or your campervan fridge—but the in-house restaurant has the advantage of being convenient when you're likely very chilled out.

One other note... Mr. Rylon is very interested in all things space-related. I heard of a nighttime stargazing tour you can do near here. They were, unfortunately, closed for a family holiday when we were in town, but if I were ever in the area again, I would try the Galaxy Gazer Astronomy Tour (www.stargazersbb.com/astronomy-tours.html#galaxy) for something different. I can say for sure that the stars were blazing as we looked at them from the campervan at night. I bet this would be an extraordinary place to observe them with an expert.

Just like that, it was the moment I'd been dreading for days. The one when we aimed our campervan toward Auckland and began the final leg of our journey before returning home. Uh-huh, I realize we're completely spoiled, having gone on a two-and-a-half-week tour of this part of the world. Plus, I'm never sad to sleep in my own bed and see my cats. But still...it's a dreadful feeling to know that the vacation you've planned and eagerly anticipated (in this case for over a year and a half) is about to be over.

The west side of the Coromandel Peninsula offers views just as spectacular as the east side.

Since I hadn't planned this part of the trip as rigidly as the beginning, and in fact had not booked a campground for our final night, we were a little unsure of where exactly we were heading. We'd been prepared to try freedom camping in the city if necessary.

It worked out beautifully, though. The nearly three-hour drive gave me plenty of time to figure out a solution in between gasping at the ocean views and panoramic landscapes from the top of ridges along the way. I popped open the Campermate app and poked around for something that had great reviews in the Auckland area.

As soon as I saw pictures of Takapuna Beach and the adjacent Holiday Park (takapunabeachholidaypark.co.nz), I was in love. The campground is steps from the ocean, with the possibility of a beachfront campsite. It's clear that this has been a longstanding getaway that used to be on the fringes of the Auckland metro area. However, the modern city has grown up around it. So this quaint little park is surrounded with bustling streets filled with markets and your choice of fantastic restaurants and attractions. Where else can you get beachfront accommodations for under $30?

With a quick phone call, we scored a spot. This ended up being another spot I feel you could easily pass several days, but we were prepared to do our best with the time we had available.

Starting with dinner reservations I'd made about a week earlier for One Tree Grill (www.onetreegrill.co.nz). In this case, I'm thrilled I already had it booked and obligation caused me to dismiss other, more convenient options. Once we rolled up to Takapuna Beach, we realized we were surrounded by fabulous eateries. If I hadn't already had the reservations, we would have certainly stayed close to "home" and tried one of those, missing out on one of the best meals of my life.

However, we hopped in an Uber—electing not to drive the campervan into Auckland, though I think there would have been ample parking if we had—and took a ride across the city to honor our dinner booking. It was beautiful at night to observe the skyscrapers, including the iconic Sky Tower, and bridges lit up along with the swarm of boats bobbing in the harbor.

The food at One Tree Grill made the effort well worth it. This "upmarket, suburban bistro featuring modern New Zealand cuisine" still holds a place in my top ten best meals of my life list. It had a modern flair with a contemporary gas fire roaring through an abstract fireplace, and all the ordering was done on tablets instead of a traditional menu. In addition to the cool factor, this was great because there were pictures of all the dishes, which made sure I selected something I would love.

Do you think I can get UberEats from New Zealand to Ohio?

Everything, from the fruity mocktail to the scallop appetizer to our lamb and beef entrees, was so good it's making my mouth water as I'm writing this. It's also making me sad that I live halfway around the word from this extraordinary restaurant. And that's even before I tell you about dessert!

I had passionfruit curd with mixed berries and dehydrated fruit powder. It was a perfect blend of sweet and tart. Mr. Rylon, who is diabetic and generally behaves himself when it comes to sweets, couldn't resist their offering of homemade chocolate truffles filled with fruit, nuts, and caramel. All told, we spent about $140 for dinner here, and I promise you that was a good value for the experience and the excellent meal.

By the time we were dropped off back at our campervan on the beach, we were as happy as our stomachs were full. Lying in bed while listening to the waves roll up on the shore as we fell asleep was something I won't ever forget.

Not too shabby! If you have to wake up on the last day of vacation, at least it's to a view like this.

DAY 18 - AUCKLAND FOODIE TOUR

Here it was. The dreaded last day. Our flight didn't leave until the evening, so we had time to squeeze in a few last things before we had to pack up, return our campervan, and head to the airport. We hadn't really seen much of Auckland other than the view out the window of our Uber or our first impressions after we'd first claimed our campervan.

To fix that, we wanted to do an organized tour and make the most of the couple hours we had left. Of course, this is another place you could spend a whole vacation by itself. There are tons of things to do in and around the city. My usual go to would be a hop-on-hop-off bus, but Auckland had more in store for us than that.

I poked around and checked several options. There was one that stood out, and made my mouth water. The Big Foody Tastebud Tour (www.thebigfoody.com/daily-tours/auckland-new-zealand-daily-tours) shows you around Auckland while letting you get a taste of the city (see what I did there?).

This tour is a small group-driven outing, similar to the one we did in Australia on the Great Ocean Road. However, on the day we attended, Mr. Rylon and I were the only guests. So we arranged to meet our guide, Colleen, at the Auckland Fish Market (www.afm.co.nz) by 9:30 that morning.

Colleen made our last day one to remember. She was welcoming and fun as she showed us around the city for four hours. She shared a New Zealander's perspective on the city. The tour was jam-packed with history, culture, and—of course—incredible food. She tailored the experience to what we were interested in and helped us find new things to try as well as leading us to places we were pretty well guaranteed to enjoy.

Our first stop was La Cigale Market (www.lacigale.co.nz). This place was bustling on Saturday morning, overflowing with smiling faces, savory aromas, and an infinite number of delicacies to try. As things caught our eye, Colleen would buy some for us to sample as part of the $125 fee we'd paid for the tour. She introduced us to local smoked meats, a patisserie, a gourmet dumpling stand, and too many other things to list.

Salash uses no chemicals or preservatives in their dry-cured products, which do not require refrigeration, making them perfect to bring home.

Next we visited Sabato, a store where chefs shop for their ingredients. Colleen had an assortment of her favorite items set out for us on a table. She had us sample everything from an amazing avocado molasses salad dressing to feijoa fruit, which I'd never even heard of before, never mind tried!

I'm not ashamed to say I really loaded up on things to bring home here, including several of the cheeses from boutique producers that we sampled. Some of them were made in small enough batches that they came from a single cow. They were so delicious I debated jettisoning some Tim Tams to squeeze more in my suitcase!

After we hauled our treasures back to the car, Colleen drove us to the waterfront area for a tour through the hundred-year-old Auckland Fish Market followed by a lovely seaside lunch. She presented us with a rich spread containing a variety of seafood featuring local green-lipped mussels.

This section of the city has been transformed recently from an industrial area to a place focused on public use, entertainment, and residences. This revitalization effort has resulted in an energetic neighborhood that you could easily spend a day enjoying.

At the conclusion of our Foody Tour, Colleen was even nice enough to drive us back to our campsite in Takapuna so we avoided having to take another Uber trip. I've enjoyed keeping in touch with her via Facebook. It's encounters like these that make me so appreciative of my ability to travel and meet people I never would have otherwise known.

If you ever are in Auckland, do yourself a favor and go on this tour!

Fresh green-lipped mussels in the Auckland Fish Market.

If I had known that we were going to stay at Takapuna and what a lovely area it was, I might have allocated more time for exploring there on our own. They, too, have a street market on Sunday mornings. From what I could see, it was vibrant and lively. Unfortunately, you just can't do it all in one trip. So I guess that means we'll have to go back sometime. Hopefully sooner rather than later.

From here we organized our luggage, cleaned out the campervan, and returned it to Maui. Within fifteen minutes, we were on our way to the airport via their shuttle.

The drive from Auckland back to Takapuna gives you a fantastic view of the city.

One thing you should consider while booking your flights is the time changes as you go. Be careful to note when you'll arrive in your next airport at their local time and what flights are available when you get there. I'm saying this because I totally screwed over Mr. Rylon (sorry!). I made sure we left New Zealand with plenty of time to cross the Pacific, then the US, and arrive in Ohio by Sunday evening because he had to go to work the following Monday morning. That was already going to be stressful for him with jet lag. I had to work, too, and actually worked on the plane a bunch, but it's not the same when you can do your job on a laptop from the comfort of your bed whenever you happen to wake up, you know?

As if that plan wasn't bad enough, it hit a snag. I scheduled us to arrive at LAX around 10 a.m. thinking we'd hop an afternoon flight back to Columbus, OH. Not so fast! What follows sounds like a bad middle school math problem, but it's real life. Unfortunately.

If you arrive on the west coast of the US in the late morning, then add time (I'd suggest a minimum of three hours) to clear customs and immigration, recheck your bags, and be rescreened at security, the earliest it's safe to book a flight out from LAX to your final destination is mid-afternoon. Leaving in the afternoon from LAX with flight time and the time change would get you to the Midwest at some ungodly hour of the morning, when the local airport is closed. Therefore, if you miss the morning flights from the west coast, you're most likely going to be stuck there until red eye flights begin around 10PM.

That means that you'll get home around 5 a.m. the next day if you're lucky. Good thing Mr. Rylon doesn't have to be at work until 6:30 a.m., am I right? Oops. Don't feel too bad for him. I did make sure to use some frequent flier miles and upgrade that last leg of the journey to first class so that he could sleep while we flew overnight.

In the end, it didn't end up mattering much because a gas pipeline broke a few days before our departure. This caused a jet fuel shortage in Auckland. In order to find enough fuel to make it across the Pacific on our flight back to LAX, we had to fly from Auckland to Christchurch where the plane refueled while we stayed onboard. Although this was supposed to be quick and painless, it wasn't. The detour ended up adding about five or six hours to our already twelve-hour flight. Thank goodness for Skycouch!

Had I tried to book us for a sooner departure, we would have ended up missing our connection anyway. I guess this is a reminder to be extra careful of scheduling when crossing multiple time zones, the International Date Line, and using multiple carriers, because otherwise you could end up stuck or missing an expensive flight.

With that, I want to say farewell. Thank you for coming along with us on our trip to Australia and New Zealand. I hope you've enjoyed hearing about our journey and, hopefully, gotten some ideas for some adventures of your own.

Up next is a budget breakdown and a link to a video I've made as a companion to this itinerary so you can see a lot of the things I've talked about for yourself.

Happy roaming!

PART V

BUDGET BREAKDOWN

So, what was the total damage?

Oh, about $16,000. Was it worth it? I enthusiastically vote yes.

Could we have done it for less (or more) money? Also yes.

In the end I think it's best if you decide what's important to you and go from there. The only real budget buster on this trip is the airfare as there aren't many ways to get around that cost. Flying basic economy, hunting for sales, and being flexible enough to score a last minute deal would be my best suggestions for reducing the price of your airfare.

Obviously, meals could be drastically reduced if you're not a foodie or need to trim the price of the trip to make it happen. Despite several of the best meals of my life, we only spent an average of $77 per day on food on the trip. I think that's pretty good for two people!

Attractions are another place you could be more cautious, taking advantage of free options instead of paid tours. I don't think it would be impossible to do the same trip for closer to $10,000 if you tried.

However you explore Australia and New Zealand, I hope you love it as much as we did.

Airfare	Attractions	Hotel	Meals	Transportation	Grand Total
$ 7,238.74	$ 3,238.07	$ 2,750.03	$ 1,399.41	$ 1,142.47	$ 15,768.72

PART VI
BONUS VIDEOS

People say pictures are worth a thousand words. Since I could only share a handful of my shots in this book, I also put together a series of three travel vlogs with video footage from this trip (and several vlogs from our other roamings).

I would love it if you would head over to my YouTube channel (www.youtube.com/c/jaynerylonbooks) to watch the vlogs which are broken down into Sydney, Melbourne, and New Zealand. Sometimes you really do have to see something to fully appreciate it.

If you like what you see I would greatly appreciate if you'd leave a like on the videos. Be sure to subscribe to my channel so you can stay up to date on future videos, too!

ABOUT THE AUTHOR

Jayne Rylon is a *New York Times* and *USA Today* bestselling author. She has received numerous industry awards including the Romantic Times Reviewers' Choice Award for Best Indie Erotic Romance and the Swirl Award, which recognizes excellence in diverse romance. She is an Honor Roll member of the Romance Writers of America. Her stories used to begin as daydreams in seemingly endless business meetings, but now she is a full time author, who employs the skills she learned from her straight-laced corporate existence in the business of writing. She lives in Ohio with ther husband, the infamous Mr. Rylon, and their cat, Frodo. When she can escape her purple office, she loves to travel the world, avoid speeding tickets in her beloved Sky, SCUBA dive, and–of course–read.

Jayne Loves To Hear From Readers
www.jaynerylon.com
contact@jaynerylon.com

facebook.com/jaynerylon
twitter.com/JayneRylon
instagram.com/jaynerylon
youtube.com/jaynerylonbooks
bookbub.com/profile/jayne-rylon
amazon.com/author/jaynerylon

ALSO BY JAYNE RYLON

ROAMING WITH THE RYLONS
Australia & New Zealand

England, Wales, Scotland, and France - coming soon!

Bonaire - coming soon!

4-EVER
A New Adult Reverse Harem Series

4-Ever Theirs

4-Ever Mine

EVER AFTER DUET
Reverse Harem Featuring Characters From The 4-Ever Series

Fourplay

Fourkeeps

POWERTOOLS
Five Guys Who Get It On With Each Other & One Girl. Enough Said?

Kate's Crew

Morgan's Surprise

Kayla's Gift

Devon's Pair

Nailed to the Wall

Hammer it Home

More the Merrier *NEW*

HOT RODS
Powertools Spin Off. Keep up with the Crew plus...

Seven Guys & One Girl. Enough Said?

King Cobra

Mustang Sally

Super Nova

Rebel on the Run

Swinger Style

Barracuda's Heart

Touch of Amber

Long Time Coming

HOT RIDES

Powertools and Hot Rods Spin Off.

Menage and Motorcycles

Wild Ride - Coming Soon!

Slow Ride - Coming Soon!

Rough Ride - Coming Soon!

Ride - Coming Soon!

Ride - Coming Soon!

MEN IN BLUE

Hot Cops Save Women In Danger

Night is Darkest

Razor's Edge

Mistress's Master

Spread Your Wings

Wounded Hearts

Bound For You

DIVEMASTERS

Sexy SCUBA Instructors By Day, Doms On A Mega-Yacht By Night

Going Down

Going Deep

Going Hard

STANDALONE

Menage

Middleman

Nice & Naughty

Contemporary

Where There's Smoke

Report For Booty

COMPASS BROTHERS

Modern Western Family Drama Plus Lots Of Steamy Sex

Northern Exposure

Southern Comfort

Eastern Ambitions

Western Ties

COMPASS GIRLS

Daughters Of The Compass Brothers Drive Their Dads Crazy And Fall In Love

Winter's Thaw

Hope Springs

Summer Fling

Falling Softly

COMPASS BOYS

Sons Of The Compass Brothers Fall In Love

Heaven on Earth

Into the Fire

Still Waters

Light as Air

PLAY DOCTOR

Naughty Sexual Psychology Experiments Anyone?

Dream Machine

Healing Touch

RED LIGHT

A Hooker Who Loves Her Job

Complete Red Light Series Boxset

FREE - Through My Window - FREE

Star

Can't Buy Love

Free For All

PICK YOUR PLEASURES
Choose Your Own Adventure Romances!

Pick Your Pleasure

Pick Your Pleasure 2

RACING FOR LOVE
MMF Menages With Race-Car Driver Heroes

Complete Series Boxset

Driven

Shifting Gears

PARANORMALS
Vampires, Witches, And A Man Trapped In A Painting

Paranormal Double Pack Boxset

Picture Perfect

Reborn

PENTHOUSE PLEASURES
Naughty Manhattanite Neighbors Find Kinky Love

Taboo

Kinky

Sinner

www.ingramcontent.com/pod-product-compliance
Lightning Source LLC
Chambersburg PA
CBHW052142110526

4459ICB00012B/1826